WAKEUP & LIVE THE FUTURE

IMMORTALS FOR A NEW SOCIETY

Book #2 In The Immortalist Series

Formally - "What if we all started to live forever?"

By Dr. Roy C. Starr, PhD, iM
Edited By Patricia A. Starr

Copyright 2016 Starrwriterpublishing 1st Edition

ISBN 978-0-9895718-2-1

i

Dedication

To my late wife I knew for 43 years, who let me see the future through the eyes of a gifted clairvoyant. Thank you Dr. PJ Starr, PhD, DM now living a parallel life in the universe.

To my current wife and editor Patricia Ann Starr, Extraordinaire

To all the immortals out there living in secret

Special Thanks to:
>
> Alan Grayson
>
> The Progressive Democratic Congressman, writer and humanitarian for his many inspiring emails and gutsy stands.
>
> The designer of the immortal human species
>
> *"The best way to predict the future is to create it." TV Commercial for BMW*

⊕Chapter 5   133

Immortal Structure 133

🍒Chapter 6   144

We the Immortal People   144

🍎Chapter 7   195

The New Rules   195

🍇Chapter 8   206

The Beginning   206

📢Epilogue   219

✍About the Author 222

Introduction

What you are about to read is either going to change the world as you currently understand it or how you live your life from this time forward. Hopefully, it may change both. If it does not do either of these minor miracles at least you will be able to dream along with the author. The first step in solving any problem is admitting that there is one. So, the world, we have a problem.

The author will address many concerns we all seem to have about the societies we live in. Some will call the solutions proposed radical or unworkable. Working out the solutions to complex problems is what living and science is all about. Traveling to distant planets was considered both science fiction and totally improbable not to long ago in history. Then we landed men on the moon and set down rovers on Mars. Not long ago, transplanting human organs from one person to another seemed impossible or ghoulish. Now we do it everyday.

Change is always a possibility and a probability. No one can design the future of a society without changing how we think. It is the job of a philosopher to analyze how we are thinking, then coming up with a solution to problems we all seem to be mired in and finally presenting a philosophy to generate change.

This book is about changing one fundamental way of how a person thinks about death. Instead of thinking and acting like a mortal, start thinking and acting like an immortal. Immortals must learn how to live in the same body forever. This leads to the need to form a new society conducive to a population of immortals.

The author creates the blueprint for a society of immortals and defines it as an immortocracy. A constitution of The People's Elysian Existence is contained in the book that addresses the current problems facing governments throughout the world. The author points out what flaws have led to failed states. Many seemingly unsolvable issues are addressed within the pages. The solutions seem idealistic but possible given the fundamental change in philosophy the book embraces. People, who have read the book, remark they would desire to live in such a society.

Patricia A. Starr, Editor

Chapter 1

The Approach

What if all that was needed was one fundamental change in the way everyone on the planet believes about death. Would it be worth writing about? Especially, if that one thing fixed the majority of the problems in the world.

Seven billion and counting and there is no plan to save humanity or the planet. There is almost no one, with the exception of a few dedicated concerned individuals, taking a stab at solving the problems we must face. We are heading towards self-extermination. Humanity may just be a blip on this planet's historical record. This fact is true, but it does not mean we should throw our hands up in the air, shrug our shoulders and shake our heads in resignation or live like there is no tomorrow. It is irresponsible and wrong to leave it to subsequent generations to solve the problems.

As a philosopher, I view the world from an objective perspective. I have no political agenda. I do not look at the world as an opportunity to gain power, fame or wealth. My perspective is devoid of personal judgement but I do have a vested interest. I live here and now. I look at the various pieces that make up individual societies or cultures and form opinions about what works and what seems to not work. I am not pragmatic. Pragmatism is the basis of compromise. It is like settling for low grade point when you should be striving for the highest.

It has been proven through time what does and does not work well in society. Unfortunately, what is not working is in power and influences everybody on the planet.

Remember that extraordinary feeling that we could make the world a better place? It bloomed in millions of hearts and then died slowly.
I remember how it felt to dream of peace, to demand justice...and expect it. How easy it was then to look forward to a day when wrongs would be righted and peace would rightfully reign. Those dreams seem like cruel delusions now. To expect better, I suppose, was foolish. -One Pissed Off Liberal (Circa 1960s)

I have a dream that needs to be shared. I am presenting answers to questions no one seems to think are solvable. It is that fatalistic point of view I am trying to put an end to. No law, regulation or philosophy is perfect. The pursuit of perfection is a worthy goal; giving up is not an option.

These are the giant steps to make such a dream come true. Plus, I need a little magic from readers like you to take this idea viral. Now is the time go into the future and out of the past.

1st Step: Use a philosophy to change how people think.

2nd Step: Give people a philosophy that makes them want to change how they live.

3rd Step: Show people how to live in accordance with the new philosophy.

4th Step: Make them understand the rewards of following a new philosophy.

5th Step: Provide powerful incentives to follow the new philosophy.

I may be a Don Quixote jousting at windmills when writing about establishing an immortalist society ruled by immortocratic laws and regulations. So be it. All genuine thought or philosophy is usually rebuked by established scholars and special interests. While they analyze the past, decry the present and prognosticate the future, I offer a new approach to the organization of an advanced mature society. A society of individuals who structure an environment conducive to living in the same physical form forever. An environment logically constructed to support indefinite life on this planet. A place where death and birth are rarities. A place where all humans are legitimately equal in all aspects of societal living. A place where no human's life is of less value than another. A place free of slavery, discrimination, object poverty, hunger, hardship, disease, and violence. A world of equal opportunity, safety, security, high quality continuing education, respectful behavior, healthful practices, innovation and economic prosperity. Why not!

> "The two most important days in your
> life are the day you were born and the
> day you find out why." - Mark Twain

Philosophy has the power to change societies, discover new worlds, invent new ways of making things, solve problems, heal wounds, fight disease and regretfully wage wars. Leadership promotes a philosophy, education teaches a philosophy and corporations tend to craft it to create an environment conducive to controlling employee behavior and marketplaces.

If you want to change a society and the hearts and minds of the individuals who make up that society, you need a unique unproven philosophy. A philosophy more enlightening than the discovery of intelligent life on another planet or an alien visit to a Dodger baseball game from another part of the universe. A philosophy that embodies entire lifestyle change like drinking the water from the fabled "Fountain of Youth" or wine from the "Holy Grail". A philosophy which would make each person effected by it stop and examine their present and future lives. A philosophy which would change the world we live in and protect the planet from manmade disaster. Finally, a philosophy which respected human life above all else and gave each person the opportunity to achieve self-actualization. Why did I want to write this book on immortal living? My reasons are somewhat idealistic and hopeful. Idealistic in its approach to societal problems and hopeful in its affirmation of the human spirit.

This philosophy has been starring us all in the face for several millennium. Millenarianism is the belief in a future golden age of peace, justice and prosperity. A doctrine which is central to the teachings of groups such as the Plymouth Brethren, Adventists, Mormons, Jehovah's

Witnesses and several other religions or similar tribal lore. All of these groups worship or pray to immortals. Believe in some type of afterlife wherein they will be rewarded for living a good life or fulfilling the written word. They also believe this eternal life after death will be in the company of immortals (angels) and that they also will become like them.

My philosophy is "Immortalism" (#Immortocracy). Don't try looking it up in the dictionary. It isn't there. Hopefully, I will put it there … forever. Society needs to boldly go there where it has never gone before. Many societies over time have tried all the other "isms". (Socialism, communism, marxism, and corporatism to name a few) They even tried hybrid "isms" by borrowing a little bit from all the "isms". The parochial "isms" have never proven to be successful over recorded time. Frankly, the most successful, as far as lasting over time, has been dictatorships or monarchies. There is little difference between those two philosophical/political entities. Both are philosophies imposed upon society by the rule of absolute power backed by brute force.

Many societies thought to be "too big to fail" have failed throughout history. Recent history has seen the demise of the Soviet State, Iraq, Libya,

Afghanistan and several others. Many other societies are at the brink of either economic or social failure. An immortocracy is designed not to fail because it uses the one philosophy that embodies foreverness.

"The stream will cease to flow;

The wind will cease to blow;

The clouds will cease to fleet;

The heart will cease to beat;

For all things must die."All things must die
by Alfred Lord Tennyson

Perhaps the greatest fear is death. It certainly is for some of us enjoying life. Sustaining a belief that one does not really die, lifts one of the great anxieties from our lives. Many people fear living a life of no meaning whatsoever or of suffering and pain.

There is certainly a case that can be made from observation that people will believe almost anything in order to hold to a belief in an afterlife. Chief of these observations is that people may with their own eyes witness death occurring, combine that with a complete lack of evidence to those same eyes of any persistence beyond death, and yet believe that there is such a persistence. A lived truth up against a mere possibility, yet for many the former cannot oust or subdue the latter. Of course, belief in a God is one of the main reasons that people feel able to believe in an afterlife. Although religious belief is not a necessary condition for belief in the afterlife, it is quite often seen as such, and for many, religious belief is sufficient condition for holding that there is an afterlife. If you think there is a God, then the blatant lack of evidence for an afterlife can be dismissed, or left unscrutinized, as it stands protected by the bigger scheme.

How many philosophers does it take to change a light bulb?

It depends on how you define 'change'.

From the invention of the light bulb, to inventing the Internet, from putting people on the Moon, to getting a rover on Mars, there is no limit to what America or the world can do when we put our minds to it. Our eagerness to innovate is one of the things that makes this time in history so great. So, why not invent a new philosophy that may inspire a better world?

Is not death a certainty?

No, it does not have to be a part of living. Death is caused by the ignorance of how to live forever. There was a time when people thought flying from one place to another was impossible. Birds and insects are born with the ability to fly and so were humans. We just had to figure out a way to do it. Just because we are programmed from birth with a deathist philosophy does not make it impossible to live forever in the same physical body we started out with at birth. How to live forever in the body you were born with is covered in my first book on physical immortality. (Titled: "How you can live 1 day after forever") This book, Wakeup & Live Forever, is about having a world, a society, to make that life more pleasant and possible.

Why did I invent a new philosophy?

Why did I invent a new philosophy? Because all the current philosophies have failed or are failing and I do not want to be collateral damage. Trying a philosophy or system of governing that has failed over and over again to achieve peace, equality, human rights, physical security, prosperity for all and social security, is the very definition of insanity. Failed states are the ultimate result of this insanity. Social unrest, hate crimes, terrorism, genocide, racism, xenophobia, religious persecution, torture and often war result in these failures. Nobody seems to be on the same page, so to speak.

The world is awash in weapons. The volume of major weapons transfers went up 16 percent between 2010 and 2014 compared to the previous four-year period, and the United States is the leading driver of the $76 billion industry. Shame on my home country. Arms supplied to one faction often end up in the hands of its enemies, making arms embargoes and targeted weapons transfers nearly impossible. And just as we have an explosion of shootings in the United States because of the availability of 300 million guns, wars are much more likely to start, continue and resist resolution because young men continue to have access to truckloads of sophisticated weaponry.

Both international and regional institutions are weak. The United Nations and regional bodies like the African Union are too weak to force combatants to lay down their weapons, too weak to provide enough peacekeepers to enforce a ceasefire, too weak to provide sufficient funds to rebuild conflict zones and ensure that strife doesn't return. Such institutions remain weak in part because: Superpowers like the United States and would-be superpowers like Russia and Turkey are determined to achieve their goals by force. The United States continues to practice an al-a-carte multilateralism, supporting only those international efforts that intersect with its national interests. As long as America continues to rule by drone, forget about a robust international rule of law and the institutions required to uphold it. They don't expect other countries to do anything other than follow the leader.

Particularism is flourishing. Ethnic nationalism and religious fundamentalism have greater appeal in the absence of strong consolidating ideologies. In many countries, ideologies such as Arab nationalism, Marxism and liberal democracy have all failed to secure peace and prosperity. It's no surprise, then, that people are turning to ideologies that are far narrower in scope and audience.

Twenty-five years ago, the Cold War ended with the collapse of the Soviet Union. Thereafter, we were supposed to embark on a path of peace and prosperity. But somehow, we lost our way. Greed got in the way.

Greed is the cancer that is killing all of us. Whether it is the military industrial complex or the environmental polluters it makes little concern to them the collateral damage they inflict. To them it is part of the cost of doing business. Profits are their only concern. The profiteers indulge themselves with luxuries and legal/illegal drugs in order to take the edge off their guilt. Materialism is their doctrine. A doctrine wherein material success and power grabbing are the highest values in life. This doctrine appears to be prevalent in western society today. How they salve their conscience is with an occasional charitable contribution to organizations that wouldn't exist if were not for the damage they caused in the first place. It is liken to giving someone who got his leg blown off by a bomb you manufactured, a pair of crutches. What a nice guy you are for not killing the poor fellow.

The triad of the destruction of a society is - Greed😷, Radicalized Religion🗣 and Depression😩.

I am not the first person to recognize these factors or to come up with a solution to eliminate the negative influence of the effects. People have risen up in the past and tried to destroy the hold this triad has on society. Most attempts have been aimed at one aspect or the other. No one has successfully tried to vanquish all three at once. Ultimately, they failed after much death and destruction. We even came up with a label for it - A Revolution (when it succeeds). Today they call it terrorism or insurrection. Like the saying goes - one man's terrorist is another man's freedom fighter.

Yes, there are true evil doers committing butchery, extermination, genocide and massacre out there that need to be stopped. Lawless warlords, who have the motivation of greed and power with the goal of creating their own dictatorship. It used to be that if you took out the leader of the movement the movement would fall apart and everybody would go home, so to speak. The old cut off the head of the snake theory. Not so anymore since the ideology is passed down to the next wannabe butcher and the former leader becomes a martyr to the cause. Revenge is added to the zeal of the members already whipped up by the warped ideology. The ideology is prominently religiously motivated with economic under pinnings. The membership (fighters or supporters) of the group have one or more of the following motivators.

Economic is a motivator because they are probably homeless, unemployed, starving, must provide for other family members so they can survive, have debt problems or simply want to get ahead monetarily by participating in plunder.

Emotional reasons (revenge) do to past circumstances wherein they, close friends, leaders or family members were killed, tortured or injured by opposition forces.

Radical religious indoctrination creates a motivator wherein they believe to be chosen to martyr themselves for not just the cause but for a god. A god that will reward them in the afterlife and a cause that will pay an economic reward to their family members. A whole body donation instead of just a kidney or some other body part. They somehow justify murdering others as way to appease their god or further their cause. It is pure insanity, suicide, desperation and wholly ineffective at achieving any goal.

There is one last part of the membership usually hidden from the press or even the core membership. This is the financiers and hired guns (mercenaries) who provide the weapons, money, training and combat skills required to sustain the group. A shadow government with its own economic or political agenda. The true head of the snake. It could be a corporation or a sovereign entity controlled by a corporation or an ideological similar organization.

It does not much matter what they call themselves to the press or how they are labeled by other world governments, they are still warlords which makes them murderers. The shadow governments are profiteers and plunders and they are also murderers. Corporate media ignores the role these warmongers have in conflicts. Glorify the sacrifices of loyal men and women of the military, somewhat ignoring the death and destruction of the societies caught up in the violence.

The reasons behind American opposition to the Vietnam War fell into several main categories: opposition to the draft; moral, legal, and pragmatic arguments against U.S. intervention; and reaction to the media portrayal of the devastation in Southeast Asia. The growing opposition to the Vietnam War was partly attributed to greater access to <u>uncensored</u> information presented by the extensive television coverage on the ground in Vietnam. For the first time in American history the media was privileged to dispense battlefield footage to the public. Graphic footage of casualties on the nightly news eliminated any myth of the glory of war. The warmongers and corporate murders learned from this mistake of losing public support. The government ended the draft and stopped allowing the filming of returning flag draped coffins or at least showing it on the corporate run news. Prior to the fall of Rome, Roman elite citizens paid volunteers (their slaves) to take their place in the Roman legions so they could avoid the horrors of war. Rome fell shortly after that because these fighters were not enthusiastic about defending a system of government in which they were disenfranchised.

Opposition forces, sometimes referred to as the good guys are often organizations and governments that are motivated by self-interest to assist non-combatants or resist the warlords. Assisting the non-combatants is a humanitarian thing to do because they are the collateral damage of the conflict. However, this also plays into the hands of the warlords because they lessen the impact of the violence and ultimately leave their assets to be plundered by the aggressors.

Refugees by leaving the area of the conflict make management of the population that much easier. Warlords don't have to feed them, provide services, guard or police them or continue having to deal with their demands. Often the refugees are forced to leave their homes, jobs, assets or businesses by the aggressors. Either by the point of a gun or physical abuse such as rape, beatings, torture or slavery. Many make the rational choice of leaving the conflict zone with some assets before they are forced to leave. Some, of course, do not have the ability to leave or figure they can weather the storm. Many of these people may and do die.

Warlords also will hold a certain amount of hostages inside cities and neighborhoods to prevent opposition forces from bombing them out of existence.

Believe it or not there are ways to eliminate or suppress warlords. However there is little or no profit in the suppression or elimination of conflicts. Greed fuels the violence from both sides. The respect for human life is totally absent from the situation. People incidentally die for greed and power because greed is rewarded with money and power. Greed is thought of as being good. A good strategy to obtain a better life. This is the essence of a flawed philosophy. Even after the conflict is over these warmongers profit from the reconstruction.

Capitalism is the philosophy that promotes greed. In fact it is the centerpiece of the philosophy. Mix in a little socialism and some democracy and you have the current superpower. Hoist a flag, sing an anthem, recite a pledge and distribute a few dividends and you create most of the wealthiest people in the world. Regrettably, less than a couple thousand out of seven billion people actually benefit from this philosophy. The rest get screwed or live a short blissful life in a comfortable retirement.

The most durable and successful societies to date were built on the principles and foundation of respectful behavior. They were referred to as "polite societies" and became strong influences in the world. Unfortunately, their influence has wained over time as greed and unbridled power has destroyed the credibility and reputation they projected. Most waged class warfare, thus a societal wedge or division occurred as a result. Greed further eroded their position as an example of acceptable behavior. When a society excludes or diminishes members of their population a society losses mutual respect for each other. The perception of the excluded class is one of envy and disgust. All respect is lost and may become totally unrecoverable. It causes the distance between the haves and have nots to widen. Lawlessness becomes epidemic. Blackmarkets, organized crime, gang warfare, and corruption in government take hold.　Ultimately, if allowed to fester, downgrades into civil war or revolution.

How do we reverse this spiral into the abyss? Leadership, education and a new philosophy are the only viable solutions.

Chapter 2
The Steps

Before I can relate further the challenges and the solutions to societies problems, I must confess that I am an American living in America. Although, unlike many Americans I have lived in other countries and traveled to many places in the world. I will try to be objective and not view problems in other parts of the world from solely an American's point of reference. I will use several uniquely American political situations that have parallels in many parts of the world. America used to be and still is a country many people in the world look up to for many good reasons. America's social, cultural and economic exports have been a big influence in other countries. Some have welcomed these influences and others not so much. Since I am writing in the English (American version) language I will use that language's references and vocabulary. My philosophy is not designed for only Americans but for the world as a whole. Lest we forget we are all on the same planet, a spaceship, which is hurtling through space.

How do we reverse this spiral into the abyss?

Leadership, education and a new philosophy are the only viable solutions to reverse this spiral into the abyss.

1st Step: Use philosophy to change how people think.

Leadership is needed that points out the problem, gets the attention of the players and puts the solution in understandable terms for all parties. Leadership needs to figure a way to level the economic playing field without plunging the economy into chaos, reverse the trend of wealth from going to the upper class or richest 2%, move profits to the workers and eliminate excessive bonus payments and perks to management. Management should never be compensated at a rate no more than five times the wage of the lowest paid worker in the company. A leader who would enact and enforce strong anti-trust and monopoly laws and make it illegal for any company to own the commons, utilities, prisons, or a public safety entity. It may be superficially cost effective or politically expedient to have private companies run government facilities or provide basic utilities such as water, power, sanitation and public transportation but it is irresponsible for us to let them own the property and natural resources associated with the implementation and production.

For example, if a farmer owns the land he farms, he solely can decide what crops to plant or not plant. He bases his decision on what he knows how to farm, the demand for his crop in the market, equipment costs, what grows well in the available soil, fertilizer, pesticide cost, and the environment he is subject to (water, sunlight, temperature, etc.). The government should not tell him what to farm or not to farm. The government should never pay him not to farm (work) or subsidize one crop over another to upset the marketplace. Why? It is his land, his labor, his investment and whether he works or not is his decision. He is not a slave or serf. The government should not control the commodity or allow some corporation to control the market but only assist the farmer with technical support and educational opportunities. The farmer is a very important member of society and his success is critical to the people he feeds. The government (the people) has an obligation to assure his success and make him as productive as possible given his resources. His success or failure ultimately depends upon him. If he needs help and asks for it, he should be given it without reservation, because we (society) need him to succeed. If he fails do to no fault of his own, we need to have his back and put him back to work for us. This makes sense on many levels and speaks to freedom.

Now, what if the farmer was a corporation, who's sole purpose of existence is to make a profit. They own the land, the equipment, and such, just like the farmer did in the previous example. They are subject to the same environmental constraints as the farmer. They study the market like the farmer and make similar decisions as to what to plant or not to plant. They have the same access to government technical support and assistance programs. The difference is that the corporation has vast financial resources, the ability to control the commodity market, influence government policy, purchase more land than one farmer can manage and ultimately absorb the farmer's property or rights. The corporation is still producing a vital resource (food in this case) to society. The difference to the consumer is invisible. What the consumer does not know is that the corporation, also owns the distribution system, the warehouses, the processing facilities, the marketing and quite possibly the retail store the product was ultimately delivered at to the consumer. Is it efficient? Yes. Profitable? Most likely. Does the consumer like what they are getting? This is somewhat uncertain   since they have no idea what it is they are really getting because of corporate secrecy. Is it fair? Ask the farmer who is now working in a factory to support his family.

The last sentence was a little too difficult for children; however, it is often the case. The point is that it does not matter if we are talking about a farmer or the water works.   The farmer once owned the land and we, the people, used to own the water works. Now a corporation owns it. We, the people, do not seem to care as long as we can take a shower or flush our toilet. It does not seem to matter to most, we the people, that we paid for the infrastructure, built the water works from scratch, and established the marketplace (the town) for the municipal water. The corporation, perhaps regulated by the local government, now can charge more than the municipality would have charged its customers for the same service because a profit is built into the cost. They can hire employees at lower rates with less benefits and give the management big bonuses. If regulation becomes a problem for them they can afford to buy elections and officials and thus the favorable environment for them to make more profits. This in turn will give them more capital to acquire adjacent municipalities. Before long they own larger and larger impact areas. We, the people, wake up one day and discover they are economic hostages (profit centers). Us, the people, lose all control of basic services and have no choice but to pay what the market demands. A market totally controlled by the corporations for the corporations. If you are waiting for the media to wake you up before it is too late, they, the corporations, own that too.

Leadership was one of the things needed to prevent a descent into the aforementioned abyss. There has to be a profound change in the way leadership is viewed by the population. It cannot be one person or an elected body. These two leadership styles, even when combined, do not function efficiently or without power struggles and corruption. The problem with leadership is the perception of the character of the leader(s). How a person looks, where they came from, how they were raised, past opinions, who they associate with, family values, sexual partners, financial dealings and a host of other voyeuristic interests. Instead of concentrating on the content of the leader's ideas or proposals people attack the person's reputation or qualifications. It is the old attack the messenger and not the message strategy used by anyone who does not agree with what is being said. Alternately, we elect leaders who play on our fears and ignorance of the facts. If you vote for someone who has made you afraid or played to your fears; then you are making a very poor choice.

Leadership is very important to assure that people understand and follow the philosophy in play. Leadership in an immortocracy is simple and straight forward. It is a knowledge based system with binary logic. Essentially robotic leadership in which questions are answered by computer and the applicable law or regulation is referenced. If you are not satisfied with the answer or need additional help a technician will assist you. If you are not satisfied with the answer then you can appeal your case to the appropriate branch of the Tree of Immortal Living (TOIL). It is hard to vilify a computer based system because it has no emotional content. (see: How do you choose members of the TOIL?)

Many things seem to be hardwired into our consciousness. Having a physical leader is one of these things. I suppose it goes to the way most of us were raised. Parents and teachers are our leaders growing up. They provide guidance, discipline and the rule of law. When we go out and get a job, we acquire a boss of some type. So it follows that we expect some type of leadership or mentor to be in our lives.

A leaderless society has never been implemented in modern history. The technology simply has not existed prior to present day. Now it is possible to implement such a system by applying the correct oversight and training. Such a system of governing would remove emotion, corruptibility and politicalized elections. A truly information based society can be created. Artificial intelligence and binary logic instead of the emotional judgements of a single person or group. Given the state of the current technology this is not a far fetched idea. The details would need to be worked out and there would be a learning curve for the general population. Navigator positions will serve to guide people through the maze of rules and regulations. Online help and system tutoring will also be available to make the system more user friendly.

Education was the second thing needed to enlighten the people. We, the people, have seen an erosion of the public education system unlike no other time in recent history. Corporate run charter schools, for profit vocational schools, and for profit colleges and universities. Student voucher programs are like writing checks to corporations to provide bonuses for their executives. The people may or may not be getting a better education for their children but one thing for sure is the parents have lost much their voice on how subjects are taught, what is being taught, from what textbooks, when and how long they are taught, why subjects are taught and who teaches their children. When they pull their children out of public school it is a voice they give up. Parents still have a choice to give their children a nonsecular education funded by the government. They had the choice prior to this voucher system but had to fund it themselves. Unfortunately, the door opened for corporate run education under the cover of helping families to financially afford parochial schools. It is important to remember that children learn how to think and behave in society within schools. If you want children to be trained to live in a corporate run world you need to give them a corporate run education. A world where greed is good and power is money. Parochial schools have their faults in comparison to public schools but they never have taught that greed was good or that money was power (at least not in my day).

In an immortocracy, education and social interaction are separated but seamlessly integrated. Traditional school buildings will no longer exist.   Curriculum will be universal, computer based, media enhanced and interactive. Custodial based teaching will no longer exist in its present form. Students will be partnered with other students from various geographical areas, cultures and ethnic backgrounds. Students will take classes over the internet with a virtual or live teacher from the safety of their homes. Physical education, music education, arts education, sports and other semi-social activities would be community based.

> "We're on the verge of a fundamentally different economy that's being absolutely transformed by the next wave of technology," Leyden said. "It will have huge ramifications on society. And someone running the goddamn country has to know that."

The last item on the list was philosophy. A battle has been waged in the philosophical arena for all of recorded history. The battle is for our hearts and minds. Philosophy, as previously stated, has the power to change societies, discover new worlds, invent new ways of making things, solve problems, heal wounds, fight disease, and regretfully wage wars. Leadership promotes a philosophy, education teaches a philosophy and corporations craft it to create an environment conducive to controlling employee behavior and marketplaces.

"The best way to predict the future is to create it." TV Commercial for BMW

The best way to predict the future **is** to create it, is how corporations control the marketplace and how we think as a society. Control the media, dole out technology slowly to maximize profits, keep people in the dark so they cannot see or rationalize what is going on and you will possess the power to shape and fleece society. The power to control how people think and react is easily abused. Manipulating people to spend their money is a corporate art form. Salesmanship is a perfectly legitimate way to earn a living. However, taking people hostage and plundering their hard earned money to pay for the necessities of living is pure greed and theft. Doing it by inducing fear is even more deplorable. There should be a special hell for the corporate thugs who enrich themselves at the expense of society.

Religions are the champions of philosophical training and education during the history of society.

Religions form societies, construct buildings and monuments, publish media, recruit members, teach children, train personnel, manage money, advertise, influence politics (internal and external), and throughout history sponsored wars and conflicts. Any honest historian would give religion credit for more than 95% of the wars waged over the last 1,500 years. Today, religion is still primarily responsible, in one way of another, for the civil wars, conflicts, unrest, and terrorist acts in the world.   Religion is the opiate of the people because it promotes a philosophy of social divisiveness and cloaks it in righteousness. Its leadership and dogma fragments geographical locations. Organized religion exerts great pressures on secular governments and constantly tries to morph the government's laws and policies into its own dogma.

When Religion causes a problem it scapegoats to God or some other deity. "It is God's will or fate would have it" Religion is the force that drives people and societies to extremes. Zealots, martyrs, missionaries, evangelicals, and other advocates of religious dogmas are promoted by organized religion. These extremists believe they are in a fight between good and evil. They view themselves as the good but are in essence the very evil they are professing to vanquish. It is no wonder they encounter resistance from people and societies who are unwilling to subscribe to their dogma.

People they approach already prescribe through either geography, birth or teachings, to their own religious or tribal traditions. They falsely believe they can convert or conquer people of different beliefs and create a harmonious world wherein all people believe what they believe and live in accordance with their dogma. They often resort to bribery cloaked in charity and humanitarian aid. They believe the world will be perfect when everyone believes the same as they profess. It will never happen but they have deluded themselves into thinking it will happen if they try hard enough to kill or convert all of those who disagree.

An interesting thing happened when I researched most of the world's religions. I was able to discover only one thing they all had in common other than dogma. It was that they all worshiped some type of immortal; a god, a deity or supreme being. They prayed to it and erected images or made icons of it. Even people who had no religious training or professed beliefs in deities stated they paid some type of homage or respect to an immortal character. It may be Santa Claus, the Easter Bunny, sprites, fairies, elves or a hundred other fictions, people confess involvement in. Many stated they believed in the ideals of the mythical character, like Santa Claus, but not in any God. I often complemented them in their respect for an immortal character, Santa Claus, that only performed good in the world and rewarded humans for being nice.

I found this phenomenalism to be both strange and enlightening. Strange in that they could not sense these immortals but believed they existed or had existed at one time on earth or are in another ethereal place. These immortals had sent ambassadors to dictate dogma or inspired mere humans to write it down for them. All of these statements professed to be from divine origin. As I wrote this book I often contemplated attributing the writing being inspired by some popular deity to give it a semblance of credibility other than a good education and research.

It seems as time passes we tend to give divine inspiration to people who write important documents, like the US Constitution. We refer to them as framers or the founding fathers and take their writings as sacred documents. We analyze each word and assign a meaning to them of our own, that of a teacher or pundits who analyzes them for us. Religious scholars make a living reading and reinterpreting scripture in order to justify dogmatic positions. Some try to put it in historical perspective, others in relation to what they think it should mean or to support their dogma.

Uncertainty happens when someone writes in vague terms, parables, ancient languages or uses examples that expire over time. Specific language like "thou shall not kill" is even subject to be interpreted in many different ways.

It could mean not to kill any living thing.
Or:
▸ not to kill just other humans
▸ to get rid of or destroy completely in large numbers
▸ to bring about the death of a fictional character to   kill someone off
▸ it means to kill off a project
▸ turn off a light
▸ turn off an engine
▸ to consume the entire contents of a bottle containing an alcoholic drink
▸ Maybe it referred to a game being played at the time the command was written to prevent the opposition from making kill shots
▸ Possibly it means not to overwhelm someone with emotion

- Not to kill with kindness
- not to kill two birds with one stone (proverb)
- not to down an aircraft, tank or a guy riding a horse.

The rewrite of that commandment should read **"No human being should do any act that may, intended or not intended, result in the death of another human being under any circumstance or authority."** There is no wiggle room in this commandment. It would preclude war, self-defense, environmental poisoning, depriving people of food or water, manufacturing weapons of any type designed to cause death, just to name a few. Too strict a commandment for you to live by? If everyone adhered to this wording of this commandment and it was codified into law, there would be peace in this world like no other time in history. It would be a safer world to live in because people would have to think about the results of their actions at home, in public places and in the workplace.

Unfortunately, we cannot count on organized religion to jump on this bandwagon and if they did the penalty would be a forgivable sin or an unforgivable sin accessed in the afterlife. Sins do not land you in jail or force you to pay a high price for violating the law in this lifetime. Of course, capital punishment would violate the revised commandment so other humane methods of punishment would have to be devised. We might have to finally address mental issues with more effort.

Punishment should always fit the crime except when it comes to causing someone's death. Merely locking someone up, that is not mentally deranged, does not address the victim(s) of the act. All it does is deprive the perpetrator of his freedom for a period of time. It does little or nothing to deter others from committing such a crime. Treating prison inmates as human beings actually works. Ascribing punishment has always been a dilemma for society and the courts. Treat people like dirt and they will be dirt. Treat them like human beings and they will act like human beings. A "principle of normality," according to which punishment is the restriction of liberty itself and which mandates that no one shall serve their sentence under stricter circumstances than is required by the security of the community.

In regard to stigma and reentry into society of the former prisoner:

"In Norway, when you're released, you're released," he replied. *"No big stigma. One guy I*

know spent 18 years in prison and is now living in my neighborhood. A normal old guy. No one cares. You find this a lot. I have many friends who've been to prison. Norwegians are very forgiving people." He paused. "Strange because we weren't always like that." This is a modified excerpt from "Incarceration Nations: A Journey to Justice in Prisons Around the World" (Other Press Hardcover; 2016) by Baz Dreisinger.

Who is currently using philosophy to control the world? (if you are familiar with political philosophies you can skip to Chapter 3)

When it comes to killing in this century, corporations are the undisputed champions. Today, the world is being overtaken by corporate fascists who seek to dictate who lives well or who becomes collateral damage. They have no armies to fight against that would force their will on society. They simply purchase governments and enslave the people by using greed, other people's money and lawyers as their guns. Silent killers hidden by the media they own. There is no Hitler, Mussolini or Franco to point to as the villain. Just a web of corporations spun around the globe catching all it can snare worth consuming. Money has become the new opiate of the people and they control the supply. No revolution can overthrow a corporation because they often fund both sides.

The only way to combat the corporate brand of fascism is with a strong counter philosophy. A philosophy designed to awaken a drugged society. Rally a society that has given in and given up. Shake up a society where the chances of having what the haves have become equivalent to the odds of winning a lottery jackpot. A society of great minds burdened by educational debt needs to be freed. Otherwise they must submit to the corporate masters to get a few crumbs of prosperity.

Here are few popular philosophies that have proven to fail over time or become mired in conflict. I need to define them for some readers so they can see the differences between immortalism and other philosophies.

The formal definition of **fascism** is a political philosophy, movement or regime that exalts nation and often race above the individual, and stands for a centralized autocratic government headed by a dictatorial leader, severe economic and social regimentation, and forcible suppression of opposition. Sound familiar?

Marxism is the granddaddy of political philosophies on the left. The child of Karl Marx and Friedrich Engels, it's the philosophy that laid the ground work for socialism and communism. But what is it? The formal definition of Marxism is the political, economic, and social principles and policies advocated by Marx, and "a theory and practice of socialism including the labor theory of value, dialectical materialism, the class struggle, and dictatorship of the proletariat until the establishment of a classless society." Much this is laid out by Marx in Das Kapital, which is a fascinating read if you are so inclined. Marxism is on the far left of the traditional left/right political spectrum.

Communism is the direct descendant of Marxism. Some of the more well-known communist states in the world are the Soviet Union (and her satellites), the People's Republic of China, Vietnam, North Korea and Cuba. Communism calls for the means of production to be owned by the government and there is limited private property. In theory, it is the final evolution of Marxism and is the perfect classless society. In practice: Well, George Orwell said it best in Animal Farm. "All animals are equal, but some animals are more equal than others."

Communism is on the far left of the traditional left/ right political spectrum.

Socialism: The middle step between capitalism and full-blown communism. The formal definition of socialism is a way of organizing a society in which major industries are owned and controlled by the government rather than by individual people and companies. So the important industries like healthcare, power, communications, transportation and other industries are owned by the state, but there is private property. Socialism is on left of the traditional left/right political spectrum.

In Socialism the rule is by economics shared and regulated by the community as a whole. A pure socialistic state does not exist in practice. It is combined with either a democracy to make a social democracy or used to transition to or from communism (Marxist Theory). It can be slippery slope to balance on. China seems to do well with its socialist state.

Democratic socialism: Social ownership of the means of production, but with a democratically elected government. The formal definition is a political ideology advocating a democratic political system alongside a socialist economic system, involving a combination of political democracy with social ownership of the means of production. The adjective "democratic" is often added to distinguish itself from the Marxist-Leninist brand of socialism, which is widely viewed as being non-democratic. We have many aspects of democratic socialism in the United States today: Public libraries, snow removal, trash pick-up, Medicare, fire protection, police protection and Social Security are just a handful of examples. Democratic socialism is on the left of the traditional left/right political spectrum.

A true Democracy is mob rule. A majority determines the fate of all whether it is a logical choice or not a logical choice. A true Democracy does not exist except in the rhetoric of politicians. A Democracy must be tempered with boundaries (rights, laws, and regulations) to keep it from spinning out of control.

In the United States:

We elect representatives that are charged to monitor the government, purpose changes, be our voice and report back to us what we need to know. Unfortunately, a majority of the people cannot name their representative(s), even if they voted for them. They cannot remember if the representative is of one political party or another. It is far sadder when you ask them who is their local mayor or town councilman. Government at the state and national level is influenced primarily by opinion polls taken by largely corporate media or special interest groups. Protests only influence politicians if they are covered by the corporate media. If violence is involved in the protest or politically inspired event the media focus is primarily on the violence and not the core issue.

This disconnect from the government to the people, it is charged to serve, has resulted in the formation of anti-government groups. There has always been discontents, racists and conspiracy theorist in society. They tend to proliferate when government fails to address social issues. The militia groups are an armed subset of so-called patriot groups who "typically adhere to extreme antigovernment doctrines and subscribe to groundless conspiracy theories about the federal government," according to the Southern Law Center.

A wave of pessimism leads capable people to underestimate the power of their voice and the strength of their ideals. The truth is this: It is the initiatives of deeply caring people that provide the firmament for a democracy.

Here's the truth: The economic and political systems of this country and many others are stacked against ordinary citizens. The rich get richer and use their wealth to buy elections and I believe that we cannot change this corrupt system. If we're serious about creating jobs, health care for all, climate change and the needs of our children and the elderly, we must be serious about the form of government we are currently using.

So far in this 2016 election, less than four hundred families have contributed the majority of all the money raised by all the candidates and super PACs combined. According to media reports, one family will spend more money in this the 2016 election than either the Democratic or Republican Parties.

This is not democracy. This is an oligarchy. Society has to pause and rethink; now is the moment. The current system of campaign finance in this country is utterly corrupt. Corruption breeds contempt for government and ultimately leads to its demise.

We can teach our soldiers what they're fighting for. We can give them ammunition in their heads to know why we fight. We had the most beautiful pearl of how to live on this Earth -- a system of government that was the first and only one to respect each individual. We had it, polished it up and the whole world began to want it and as their desire became urgent we changed the political goals of the entire world -- until we did the dumbest thing we could and stopped teaching it.

National Socialism, aka the Nazis: This is not socialism no matter what anyone tells you. It is a fascist-based philosophy. The formal definition is the ideology and practice associated with the 20th century German Nazi Party and the Nazi State as well as other far-right groups. It's usually characterized as a form of fascism that incorporates scientific racism and anti-Semitism. National Socialism is on the far right of the traditional left/right political spectrum.

Islamofascism: Is this really even a thing? Formally it is defined as an ideology promoted by a small minority of Islamists, the aims of which are to establish Islamic orthodoxy and to resist western secularism. However, many critics are dismissive. Daniel Benjamin brands it as "meaningless." Norman Finkelstein calls it a "kosher-halal" throwback version of the "vacuous" old leftist epithet "fascist pig." Paul Krugman calls it a "figment of the neocon imagination," and Angelo Codevilla states that it "betrays an ignorance of both Islam and Fascism." It appears that Islamofascism is something our conservative friends made up as a bogeyman to replace the former Soviet Union. I have no idea where this made-up thing goes on the traditional left/right political spectrum.

An Aristocracy, an Oligarchy, Plutocracy and Fascism is rule by the rich or well-born and is a form of a dictatorship. A few rule the majority at their whim. In a Dictatorship one person rules usually with an iron fist. Benevolent Dictatorships have and do exist on a small scale but tend not to last longer than the span of the dictator's life or the span of their control. I again have no idea where this reality goes on the traditional left/right political spectrum since it depends on who or what body is in charge.

A **Theocracy** is a form of government in which a deity is officially recognized as the Civil Ruler and official policy is governed by officials regarded as divinely guided (by a fictional immortal), or is pursuant to the doctrine of a particular religion or religious group (invented by a mortal man or men). It is another form of a dictatorship, akin to fascism, with plausible denial built-in. It is just another

Political Faction, which is a group of people with a common political purpose, with inflexible rules (dictates). Quite possibly the most destructive and radical of all forms of governmental control. If Adolf Hitler of Germany and Benito Mussolini of Italy had been religious clerics instead of elected officials we all would be all under theocratic rule. History should teach us that religion and politics is a volatile mix. Historically, more wars, violence, loss of life and senseless destruction of the environment has been caused by one religion or another since the beginning of civilization than any other from of governing of mankind. If you want to fear one thing in this convoluted world we live in, then it should be some type of religion or any religion for that matter. God is not a benevolent dictator. God is the other type of dictator who must rule with an iron fist. Dictators die or are overthrown. Gods are immortal and cannot be overthrown or appealed to for a change of policy (unless administered by a benevolent Pope or some other cleric). Religions are inherently immune or resistant to change. Religions tend to fight amongst themselves for the domination of the minds of mankind. Every religion has the idea that they have the only true god (religion) and that theirs is more powerful than yours; most are willing to sacrifice life to prove it.

I am not anti-religion, anti-god or anti any belief system. I am even not anti-gun; but I am anti-ammunition. If you put a loaded gun to my head I would believe whatever you would want me to believe. I am very much pro-life; especially my own. It would be wise for anyone to engage in a lifestyle of self-preservation.

A **Corporatocracy** is a co-opted form of governing people and property for profit without regard to human rights or morals. It is the current system that is manipulating all other forms of governing for dominance. It is a cancer seemingly without a cure that is spread by media and advertising. It controls by purchasing and controlling what humans need to survive, bribing officials, and ruling marketplaces. It is the primary cause of social unrest throughout the world. It creates an ever widening gap between the haves and have nots. It sponsors genocide and strong military regimes. In regard to employees,   money goes to the company instead of the inventor. On the traditional left/right political spectrum it manipulates both sides and the center for power and money.

The rich keep getting richer, and by next year, just a handful of the upper-class will have accumulated more than half of the world's wealth.

A new report released by Oxfam warns that this deepening global inequality is unlike anything seen in recent years. Using research from Credit Suisse and Forbes' annual billionaires list, the anti-poverty charity was able to determine that the richest 1 percent of the world's population currently controls 48 percent of the world's total wealth.

If trends continue, Oxfam predicts that the most-affluent will possess more wealth than the remaining 99 percent by 2016, The New York Times reported.

Drill down the numbers even more and you'll learn that the 80 wealthiest people in the world possess $1.9 trillion, which is almost the same amount shared by some 3.5 billion people at the bottom half of the world's income scale.

Thirty-five of the lucky 80 were Americans with a combined wealth of $941 billion. Germany and Russia shared second place with seven uber-rich individuals apiece.

Not surprisingly, the richest were titans in the finance, health care, insurance, retail, tech and extractives (oil, coal, minerals and gas) industries and they paid fortunes to lobbyists to maintain or increase their riches. Seventy of the world's wealthiest were men and 11 members of the elite 80 simply inherited their wealth.

"Do we really want to live in a world where the 1 percent own more than the rest of us combined?" Oxfam executive director Winnie Byanyima said in a letter. "The scale of global inequality is quite simply staggering and despite the issues shooting up the global agenda, the gap between the richest and the rest is widening fast."

In 2015, more than 2,500 of the world's rich and powerful flew to Switzerland on hundreds of private jets to attend the World Economic Forum. There they chatted about the financial markets and economic trends while eating the finest food and staying in Davos' five-star hotels.

It may be too late to reshape a society infected by the cancer of corporate greed. Corporations only fear one thing just like all the other forms of rulership has feared throughout the centuries. They fear the people. It is why they live in guarded and gated compounds. The modern day equivalent to the medieval castles. Protected by well paid mercenaries and corrupted governments. People fear them because their jobs and livelihood depend on them. This is Serf Mentality; which is the concept that essentially refers to the acceptance, by the people, of the culture or doctrines of the enslaver as intrinsically more worthy or superior. People accept their plight and roles in society without question or dissent because it is what they inherited at birth and were taught in schools.

> "Fighting corruption is not just good governance. It's self-defense. It's patriotism." ~Joe Biden

You cannot overthrow corporations like governments. Like the proverbial snake that grows a new head if you cut it off, corporations just keep growing new heads. A person might as well try to successfully try to abolish a religion. May you have good luck at being successful in doing the near impossible. Religions just splinter into factions with reformed dogma.

The only way to fight corporations is to nationalize them. **Nationalization** is the process of transforming private assets into public assets by bringing them under the public ownership of a national government, state, county or city. Industries that are usually subject to nationalization include transport, communications, energy, banking and natural resources. It would be a good start and it has been done with some success in the past but only by dictatorships and quasi democracies. Often the leadership is assassinated or deposed by corporate mercenaries.

Nationalization has to start at the municipal level of government and not from the top levels of government to be successful. It must be communities taking back control of their vital resources. If someone else owns the well you drink from you have to ask their permission to drink.

Communities also need to take back the local media who have been relegated to covering local sports, fundraisers, church news and social news. Public broadcasting supported solely by money from all the people and not advertising, endowments or the government is the best method. An argument can be made that government funding of public broadcasting is rationally money from all of the people. Unfortunately the governing body that provides the funds attaches strings to money which would be interpreted as undo oversight of reporting.

These topics are better served now by social media and email campaigns. Weather, fashion pieces, sports scores, and traffic reports are not news and information; just filler. People should be more interested about the price of orange juice and gasoline than what the stock market averages did that day. Real investors who gamble in the stock market already know the daily numbers before normal consumers here them on TV. There are media channels dedicated to all these niche markets.

It is not beyond reason to summarize stock market number reporting is, in itself, a way to manipulate small investors into making poorly thought out sells or purchases of stock. The gamblers know movement is the key to profit and loss in the stock market.

Let local media refocus on local issues and write or talk about their own unbiased take on national, state, and international news as it effects the communities they serve. Publishing editorials and opinions is not enough. Real news and factual information examining these editorial opinions needs to be given. Publishing news and information that the corporate media feels will increase advertisement revenue is laziness and self-serving. News cannot be selectively reported to enhance its entertainment value.

An educated and well informed public is what scares the corporations, by far, the most. Transparency does not exist in the corporate world and is severely limited in national government. In the corporate world everything goes on behind closed doors. In government it is shrouded in secrecy. The government is of the mindset that the people cannot handle the truth and decide what is right or wrong. Corporations only care about profits and an image that effects profits.

> *"An educated citizenry is a vital requisite for our survival as a free people,"* said Thomas Jefferson.

What we as a society have been subjected to for too long has been a persistent effort to make sure the citizenry is anything but educated. This was done to accrue political power for the enrichment of the few at the expense of the many.

So there you have it. A very brief tutorial on many of the political philosophies. It looks like quite a mess to clean up. It is no wonder no one puts on overalls, gloves and hip boots to wade into the problems. Later, once this book is published, I will don my kevlar vest and Nomex flame-resistant suit to weather the storm of critics and naysayers. I do not claim to have all of the answers or even all of the questions, but I think this book should stimulate serious thought if not constructive criticism.

Chapter 3
Laying the Foundation

"A lifetime isn't forever, so take the first chance, don't wait for the second one! Sometimes, there aren't second chances! And if it turns out to be a mistake? So what! This is life! A whole bunch of mistakes! But, if you never get a second chance at something you didn't take a first chance at? That is true failure." — C. JoyBell

What is an Immortocracy?

An Immortocracy is common sense rule by highly qualified immortals for immortals and by immortals. The qualification to not to govern but to administer and oversee the actions of government. Intelligent and compassionate people to implement the basic precepts of immortality and make changes as technology and society evolves. They are caretakers not rulers. There is no one leader but a group of specifically chosen immortal administrators based on their qualifications to function in that position. Wise men or wise women if you need to title them. People who are not just inflexible technocrats or idealists, but people with compassion and good judgement. All branches of government must have at least three equally qualified humans in control that act like judges or group administrators. All of them must agree with any decision or change made based on the objective facts. Decision-making can be regarded as the cognitive process resulting in the selection of a course of action among several alternative possibilities. Every decision-making process produces a final choice that may or may not prompt action. Any immortal can seek redress to restore balance or improvement in a situation with an appropriate branch of government with a question or a constructive idea. Leadership is by a computer based binary logic system. A knowledge base which is accessible by all citizens created by each branch of the TOIL.

The Branches of the Tree of Immortal Living (TOIL)
Justice
Transportation
Natural Resources
Land Use
Housing and Urban Development
Waste Management
National Food Policy
Public Safety
Education
Social Security & Economics
Media Affairs
National & International Relations
Technology and Defense
Arbitration
Oversight and Ethics

All branches of the Tree of Immortal Living (TOIL) have the ability to make regulations, set forth guidelines, listen to appeals and render decisions within the span of control of there respective branches. Any other branch of the TOIL may appeal regulations set forth by another branch to the Arbitration branch which must resolve any conflicts between the branches by amendment or nullification.

Only one set of laws and regulations for all geographical locations within the TOIL's span of control. What is legal or not legal is the same for each location, one level of government, law enforcement and inherent jurisdiction.

The Arbitration Branch is composed of elected heads of each branch by the branch members. The branch head who represents the decision to be arbitrated acts as the defendant and the branch head who brought the challenge to the decision as the plaintiff. The arguments are made by the parties and the other branch heads question and ultimately decide the case by mediation or unanimous vote.   All meetings and information obtained by any branch of the TOIL are open and public. No secrets or omissions from the public record. Public comment or input is by written word or oral video. The public may not address the any branch of the TOIL in person without the consent of the branch members.

TOIL branch members are drafted or chosen by a committee of Academics, Philosophers and

Regional Judges. Branch members serve four year terms and can volunteer to serve additional terms after being out of service for four years or more. Any person can volunteer and apply to be a member of a branch who has the educational and/or experiential requirements to serve in that capacity. No other requirement other than the pledge to serve without prejudice towards any race, gender, belief system, or status is needed to qualify a person to serve. A branch member is not allowed to profit in any manner from being of service. Branch members are provided a base salary, housing, budgeted expenses, a staff of five assistants chosen by the member and a functional office in the branch building.

Ideas, technological developments, relative questions, problems to be solved are the duties of the members of each TOIL branch. Society has complex and serious problems to address and solve in every discipline.

The Oversight and Ethics branch of the TOIL investigates allegations of wrong doing by members of the TOILs and those administrators appointed by them. Any citizen can make written allegations to this TOIL.

No single branch of government can efficiently handle a broad range of issues confronting a society. Such a method is prone to grid lock, influence peddling, bribery and a lack of confidence in by the governed. It simply does not work in a modern complex society. It leads to chaos, rebellions, hardships, inefficiencies, waste, fraud and abuse. No government or ruler can survive this method of operation over the span of a millennium or even the span of a decade in some countries.

An elected representative government is window dressing and should go to the scrape heap of political ideology. Society needs solutions, adaptability to change, intelligent design and competent supervision.

Think of it this way ... If you wanted someone or a group to build you a home, you would select the best available professionals to perform the task. Especially, if you were footing the bill. You would expect them to listen to your requirements, provide guidance, draw plans, comply with building codes, spend your money efficiently, apply the latest technology, supervise the building, use competent people to perform the work, test and inspect all systems and do it all without creating problems for you or for your neighbors.

Is that too much to expect? Of course not.

Operating a government should be akin to operating a large high rise hotel. Hotels require professional management and qualified personnel who understand how to operate and maintain a complex structure while serving the needs of their guests. Each guest needs to be treated with the same quality service and afforded privacy and respect regardless of their status. This is what people want from their government. When needs are met, safety is assured, things run smoothly, and a reasonable cost is associated, people are satisfied with the hotel and therefore their government.

As a society we have enacted a myriad of laws, codes, regulations and guidelines. Some essential, some significantly flawed, some partisan, some corrupt, some discriminate, some unneeded and some we should repeal or amend.

There are three main problems with all of these enactments. First, there are too many and too complex for any one person to understand or apply. Second, they are not consistent or may not exist from one geographical location to the next. Third, they are enacted politically and not scientifically in far too many cases. What is against the law in one location is legal in another for no logical reason other than the politics. Examples are marriage laws, gaming laws, mineral rights, traffic enforcement, public safety, food safety and educational standards to name just a few. Some laws are to prevent certain businesses and others to facilitate certain businesses. Enactments to allow detrimental businesses to operate in an irresponsible manner and cause pollution or damage to the environment. Other enactments to keep businesses out of certain communities to maximize property values. All of it is political in nature and highly susceptible to bribery and corruption. There is little problems with logical professional community planning to make a harmonious atmosphere to live and work in for the community. Some geographical locations are better suited for certain types of businesses and should be restricted to those locations based upon facts and science not politics.

Every population area needs basic utilities and services to be functional. They also need some type of economic engine to employ the labor that the population represents such as; tourism, industry, manufacturing, agriculture, teaching or a combination of several types to create jobs. A city, town or village is a society codependent on each member within its span of control. Each one of these entities are a part of an even larger state or country which is interconnected with the entire planet. We are all riding on the same spaceship called earth. Thus we all have a part to play and the associated responsibility to keep the ship in good shape.

A revamp of how societal members are educated and involved in the operations of the day to day living is of the upmost importance. Experience based education must go hand in hand with classroom instruction in the workings of day to day operation of a mature society. Advanced citizenship involves hard work and must involve all the population; even if it is only up close observation of a trained professional.

In an immortocracy, corporations, if they exist, will not be allowed the rights of private citizens. In fact they should not exist at all in an immortocracy. In the meantime, corporate meetings, policy and written correspondence must be open to the press, employees and the public. Corporations will not be allowed to avoid commenting on investigative reports and must confirm or substantially deny any allegations of misconduct.

Unlike private citizens corporations will not be allowed to not explain their actions when legal action is pending against them. People working for corporations will be credited for inventions and hold public patents for them in trust with the corporation for no more than five years. Patents will not be issued on the altering of living organisms, or the cells or seeds they originate therefrom. On going research will be confidential until it is patented and approved for sale to the public or consumed by non-volunteers.

In an immortocracy, various TOILS (Tree Of Immortal Living) will set out goals for collectives, co-ops or individuals to achieve and will create monetary incentives. The profits will not be taxed nor will the gains or losses of investors or owning employees incur any tax or relief from taxes. Investors will be shareholders but have no voice in the management or operation of the business. Investors are silent partners who get a wage (dividend) yearly based what a working individual receives each year on average.

For example: The collective has 100 employee owners and 100 investors who contribute in capital the wage of the average employee. One employee on average earned 10,000 credits for working plus benefits. So the investor invested 10,000 credits in the collective. At the end of the year the collective earned 1,000,000 credits in net profit. The employees and the investor share equally in the profits. 1,000,000 / 200 = 5,000 credits for each employee and investor.

🍓Chapter 4
FAQs

How does an immortalist society deal with immigration situations?

Immigration from one geographical or geopolitical location to another has been a global concern. The two primary reasons people want to immigrate from one place to another are economic and environmental reasons. Economic reasons are the need for a job paying a fair wage to support themselves and their family members in manner better than they have been experiencing where they are currently located. Environmental reasons are situations such as political instability, war, violence, famine, natural disasters, inadequate housing and health threats.

Economic reasons have been the problem since the primal existence of society. Most of the problems in the ancient world were slavery and wars. This has not changed very much since ancient times. When an individual cannot earn enough money for his or her labor to support a modest lifestyle or stave off hunger, then the person must either submit to earning slave wages or relocate to a location they anticipate making a better living wage. It is that simple, in most cases, when you boil down a variety of compelling reasons given by the worker. Not many people move from the geographical location they were born or raised in just because they want a change of scenery. Uprooting a family, physically moving from one place to a distant other place, finding new employment, possibly having to learn another language, establishing a new residence and making new contacts is not one considers doing on a whim. Also there is the monetary cost of relocating, which precludes many from making such a move unless forced to by external events. They are so poor that they cannot make such a move because they are trapped by the slave wages that barely keeps them alive. They hope for an opportunity or a change to happen over time. The lottery of the proverbial slave laborer rarely pays out. These are the invisible fences that keep them prisoners.

The cure for this immigration situation is simple but rarely administered because of bigoted extreme greed and a lack of governmental leadership. Often these two factors are strongly influenced by the systemic use and the condoned behavior of corruption. Governmental leadership is cooperating with the power of the monied interests to gain a financial advantage of their own and to secure their own welfare. It goes to the saying that money corrupts and power corrupts absolutely or is it absolute power corrupts absolutely. Either way the result is the same. A lack of an adequate minimum wage and a fair distribution of labor is the cause of the effect of poverty.

"There was a really bad drought that lasted 3 years. People can survive a year, maybe two. Three [years], forget it," said Cane, noting that the drought destroyed the livelihoods of many Syrians and pushed the region to a tipping point. "You had this pretty stable, functioning agrarian society everybody left and went to the outskirts of the cities where there was nothing for them and a government that did nothing."

The Syrian conflict began in March 2011, with protests against the regime of President Bashar Assad. The Assad government responded with a violent crackdown on protesters and four years later various armed factions -- ranging from moderate U.S.-backed rebels to the extremist Islamic State group -- are fighting for control of the splintering country. An estimated 200,000 people have died in the conflict and the United Nations estimates that 7.6 million have been internally displaced.

"We're not saying the drought caused the war," Richard Seager, a climate scientist at Lamont-Doherty Earth Observatory and another co-author of the paper, said in a statement. "We're saying that added to all the other stressors, it helped kick things over the threshold into open conflict."

Military and national security experts have already warned that climate change can contribute to conflicts around the world, in many cases exacerbating already existing conditions. But while most predictions about climate change's impact on conflict look far into the future, this latest research finds it is already happening, at least in the case of Syria. Along with the fact, the country was made awash in arms by the world arms dealers. The warlords kindled the flames and became the only benefactors of a cruel war.

How would an immortalist society change war in the world?

The answer is simple; change how people think about dying.

This is one of the most famous war photos of all time. Famed photographer Robert Capa took this picture at the moment a bullet hit this soldier in the Spanish Civil war. The intimate yet tragic photo showcases the human cost of war. It brings home that war isn't just about ideals, it's fought with real people who bleed and die for a cause they may or may not understand.

Why is there such a high suicide and PTSD rate amongst members of the military forces?

The answer is quite simple but the solution not so much. When you hire and train someone to kill without remorse you are going against the basic instinct of the animal you have trained. Other than psychopaths, no human kills another human without remorse.

Animals rarely kill members of their own species without motivation. Humans are not territorial animals. Humans are emotional animals. They kill with emotion. Either they are angry or fearful when they kill. Angry killing is cause and effect behavior. Someone kills your friend, for example, and you react by killing them (sometimes the case in a war zone) in a fit of rage and justification. Fearful killing is when someone tells you, for example, that if you don't kill the enemy, who they select, they will ultimately kill, you, your family, friends or neighbors. Fearful killing is what the trained military person is all about. His or her fears are deep rooted, wrapped in a flag, and nurtured by his or her's training. They are taught not to question orders because it is a matter of survival in combat.

However, one day they are forced to kill by their situation in accordance with basic training. Going against their animal instincts and perhaps naturing as a child when they were taught not to kill or even cause harm to another person. The images of the experience are burned into their conscious minds forever. Images that cannot be erased and only fade with many years of time. This is the essence of and cause of suicide and PTSD among people serving in war zones. Angry killing rarely causes PTSD but fearful killing definitely does. Especially when it happens repetitively over a long time (multiple deployments to war zones).

Now, these warriors return to a society where they must adjust to the loneliness and lack of meaningful employment. Loneliness because their comrades are no longer surrounding them and the families they left behind have not changed. Families they intentionally removed themselves from when joining the military. Their friends and people they dated or married have moved on. Top that off with a feeling of regret for having made a sacrifice for an extremely dysfunctional society and you have the recipe for deep depression. Depression that gets treated with drugs and/or alcohol. Good men and women in their relative youth are lost to society forever by suicide. These people were volunteers not draftees. A tragedy of an unnecessary and greed motivated wars and conflicts. Shame on society for allowing this to happen over and over again.

This indelible image is from the Korean War and was taken in 1953. It's a fleeting moment that shows the humanity of a man who has spent weeks or months in a war zone. But all that blood and death is temporarily forgotten as he feeds a kitten. It's a reminder that these men that are sent to fight battles, are made of the same emotions that all people share.

The near perfect military weapon is the robotic killer like a drone, which is a machine without emotions. Drones do not commit suicide, defect, or come back home with PTSD (Post Traumatic Stress Syndrome). Pilots rarely experience PTSD because they do not see close-up the deaths they inflict. The mind somehow views death and violence on television, in the movies and in video games as not being real or traumatic.

The problem with wars during these times is that the enemy is rarely easily identifiable or is the field of battle well defined. Urban gorilla warfare is common name for it. Noncombatants are usually nearby or in the line of fire. It is difficult to discern the soldier's target and thus everything becomes a threat. This makes for many targeting mistakes. It also leads to a shoot first and ask questions later mindset. Police officers are also faced with this dilemma on occasions. Combat veterans sometimes are not the ideal choice for police work because of the experience of urban warfare.

Why discuss this societal problem in the context of this book about immortal philosophy and living?

First off, immortal humans would never entertain the idea of killing another human for the logical fear of being killed themselves. Mortals only kill mortals. A nice side effect of immortalist philosophy is that no one wants to die for any reason; let alone a political, economic or a religious reason. They fear death by the illogical behavior of a mortal, their own ignorance or stupidity and relatively nothing else.

If you hand a weapon to an immortal and tell them to go kill they would take the weapon and run as far away as possible from the fight and then destroy the weapon. If you point the weapon at the immortal and threaten to pull the trigger if they do not do as you say, you can bet they would most likely try to persuade you not to shoot them or anyone else. No draftee will fight for long and will desert at the first opportunity. This is a proven fact.

A person should and will defend to protect his own life and the lives of the people he loves. The person is merely defending to survive and will eliminate the threat to his life and those lives he values as much as his own. Not necessarily by taking up arms being the first choice but the last resort.

One of the basic rights that every human must have and every government should guard against being abridged is the right to life. No government, corporation, religious organization or other person has the right to your life. A right is a moral principle defining and allowing a person's freedom of action in a society. A man has to have the right to his own life. All other rights flow from that fundamental right.

Secondly, immortals would find a way to avoid conflict or situations that would cause them harm. They understand that the only way they can die is by invoking fear or anger in another human or by doing something else stupid to cause their own death.

Wars, violence, and conflict or any kind is strictly considered irrational behavior and not something an immortal would engage in. In a society governed by immortalist principles, machines of war, violence and killing would cease to exist. Humans would feel reasonably safe and would concentrate their efforts in making the planet and the living environment as safe and comfortable as humanly possible. Building defenses against humans is counterproductive. There is no wall high enough and no armor strong enough to stop an irrational human.

Why do mortals commit suicide?

There are many reasons for the cause of depression that leads to suicide. No one really wants to commit suicide. Many who try and fail will tell you it was a bad idea at the moment and wish they had not attempted to kill themselves. Experts in the field will state it was an attempt to bring attention to the individual's problems. This is substantially true in most cases. Suicide to an immortal is not something to contemplate because it goes against everything they are trying to accomplish in living.

It may seem simplistic or harsh to state that suicide is giving up on living. Living is hard work. Earning a living takes courage and determination. Dealing with everyday problems is often difficult and depressing. Suicide is the cowards way out of living. Besides you can never know what the future may bring.

> We take time to treat sprained ankles.
> It's the same way with minds. —
> Unknown

Change your focus from dying to living like an immortal. Immortals figure they can out-live any problems or other people for that matter. Bury your problems in the past but not your body. Life is a series of "do overs". Death cannot be undone. There are seven billion other people in the world that you have not met. Don't cheat yourself out the experience of living. Everything in life is temporary no matter what you may think. Tomorrow the sun will rise, the water will flow, the wind will blow and the sun will set again. This is the cycle of life.

Why are our youth becoming disillusioned with the world?

Pragmatism, depression and the insane reality that is the society we are currently living in are the reasons.

Pragmatism is recognizing the hopelessness of not being able to achieve lofty goals and having to settle for something that makes you want to give up or throw-up. Depression is the result of the frustration of not sensing any real progress in your personal life. A better word for depression is stagnation. A feeling of not going anywhere at a very slow pace.

Maturing young people want to feel like their lives have meaning beyond what is expected by their parents and teachers. They are seeking mentors or causes that will make them feel important and involved. They watch and listen to what is going on around them and latch onto whatever peeks their curiosity and/or stimulates a desire to fight for or against a cause. They either seek approval or disapproval. Whichever gives them the most sense of belonging and worth is what they want to achieve. Young people all over the world have taken up arms to fight for or against particular causes. Generation after generation we have witnessed this phenomenon with the immature adults. Old men do not fight wars for a reason and that reason is not physical fitness. Maturity usually gives insight into the fact that violence resolves nothing and only begets more violence. You cannot destroy and enemy or fully defeat it. You must resort to diplomacy and compromise to gain a victory for both sides. Peace has always been more difficult to achieve than war.

Are immortals risk takers?

A society wherein safety is a primary concern, risky behavior would cease to exist. Creating living environments safe from the forces of nature and accidental encounters is the best way to allocate resources. As an example; transportation systems would be designed to be as safe as technology would allow. Engineers would design cars that could not crash into other cars or objects and if they did the passengers would likely survive. The same for trains, planes, boats, and other forms of transportation. Robots would do tasks considered dangerous or endangering. It may sound like a little less than exciting world to the extreme sports fanatic, but trust me that inclination for an adrenaline rush would fade in an immortalist. Only a mortal has the mindset (deathist philosophy) that death is inheritable or inevitable. Mortals flirt with death because they know, in their mind, that they are going to die. Strange as it sounds they have a curiosity about what death is like. Going to the edge is liken to dangling over the edge of an active volcano or jumping out of a perfectly good airplane.

Some people would wrongly fear or oppose strong safety regulations or feel their individual rights to engage in unsafe behavior are being denied. My mother had a saying about wearing a warm coat to walk to school on a freezing winter day. She said: "A fool and his body heat are soon parted". When someone engages in unsafe behavior, on their own voluntarism, that endangers only themselves it is either by stupidity or ignorance. If the case is ignorance then a warning and an explanation is sufficient. When it endangers others it is lawlessness.

In the case of stupidity, a person has the right to his own life and safety and should be prepared for the consequences of their action. When an individual understands the possible consequences of their actions and still performs the act, he or she may only do harm to themselves or property; however, it is still crime against society since the outcome of the act is uncertain and may have caused injury to another person then or in the future.

For example an individual drives a vehicle recklessly and crashes it into a tree. They are the only person injured and the vehicle belongs to them. A stupid act with predictable results. Is it lawlessness? Yes, it is and the individual should be cited by law enforcement. Why? Because the person could have injured someone else, either when the act was committed or after the fact when someone responds to the accident is injured. Insurance should never cover the stupidity, only the effect it had on others.

Courage is making your world gun free!

What are some of the major challenges to living an immortal life?

War, Weapons, and Violence ...

More than once an unhinged person slaughtered innocent people for no rational reason. They walked into a store and bought an assault rifle, a semiautomatic handgun and loads of ammunition or strapped on a suicide vest. Why? Because they could and we as a society let him. It is our fault for making gun purchases, explosive manufacturing and possession legal. The blame is ours to shoulder. We are weak and not strong enough to make the changes in the way we allow guns and explosives to be propagated throughout our country and the world for that matter. This is one problem that a society of immortals needs to change and must change in order to survive.

It is time to put the warlords out of business along with all of the supporting arms dealers and manufacturers who finance their agenda. It is corporate greed that fuels the bribes to keep common sense laws from curbing gun proliferation. It is a simple good business practice for these companies to keep guns legal and fear rampant. The gun violence and gun suicide deaths are just collateral damage they can turn a blind eye to. They hide their greed behind a duped membership of gun owners. Every time some mental case becomes unhinged they quietly celebrate by buying another corporate jet. They do not even bother to send flowers to the traumatized victims.

They hide behind the sick and twisted words that guns don't kill people, people kill people ... or more guns in the room would have minimized the number of people killed. The last one is pure greed on their behalf to sell more deadly product.

How much more can we tolerate before we act and do what is basic common sense. Background checks, banning immigrants from certain countries, arming the population, open carry and other half measures do not address the real problem with guns, ammunition and explosives. It is past the time to act using the only possible remedy to give our society a chance of living in peace without hyper fear. Stop producing, selling and trading weapons of mass killing.

Eighty-Eight is the current 2016 average number of gun deaths each day in the United States. 88 is more deaths than the US Military Deaths each day in the **Vietnam War, Korean War, American Revolutionary War, War of 1812, Iraq War, Afghanistan War (to date), and the Philippine-American War** which comes to a **combined total of (87.37)** per day. If this trend continues for all of 2016 then **31,977 people will die** this year by a gun. By the end of 2017 guns will have killed more people in the US than the total US Military Deaths during the entire Vietnam War from **1961-75 (58,209)**. What should we do? Erect a memorial to their families? Their voices of protest have been silenced forever by a gun. They will never experience living forever. Someone has to speak for them. The least we could do is bury the gun that killed them in the same grave so it will not kill another.

I am sorry this is not a problem that we, as an immortalist society or any society, can live with. This problem needs to be addressed. Our world society needs to grow up and be more mature like China and other countries. Put away our toys for good and act like adults. Guns are for killing things. They are not toys, status, recreation, a replacement for law enforcement, problem solving or a way to deal with your depression or fears.

The warlord's spokespersons like to make light of the " 88 gun deaths a day" in the US. What do they think is an acceptable number? 50? 25? Wait until someone a member of their family cares about dies as result of a discharge of a gun. Maybe then one will be enough or too many for them. I may be an optimist to think there is something to be done to stop or slow the problem of gun violence and gun murder/suicide, but I do not have my head in the sand and waiting for the world to end before doing something about it.

Adults with guns entertainment media and organizations promoting arming everyone needs to stop influencing young people to become gun owners. Common sense changes need to happen.

Gun control does not work and this fact has been proven in mature societies in other parts of the world. Incremental changes just prolong the problem and give the death merchants more time to make more money. Removing guns from the equation is the only solution proven to be viable. Any recovering alcoholic will tell you that the only way to stay sober is to not drink alcohol, stay out of bars and change your friends. So here are the twelve steps to break a societal addition to guns.

This is what will eventually need to happen in the US and many other immature places as it has in other countries:

1. Gun and ammunition manufacturers will be restricted to making guns and

ammunition only for the military or law enforcement.

2. Gun retailers will liquidate and close their doors.

3. Gun shows will no longer be allowed.

4. Private sales of guns and ammunition will be prohibited.

5. Guns, military items and ammunition will not be allowed to cross national borders in either direction. America and other countries will permanently be out of the arms business.

6. Local government and law enforcement will sponsor gun and ammunition buy back programs to allow owners to dispose of unwanted firearms.

7. No open carry will be allowed by private citizens.

8. All guns and ammunition must be registered and stored with local law enforcement.

9. Hunting will only be allowed by license and in the presence of a certified guide. Individuals who hold hunting permits can apply to purchase and store, with local law enforcement, firearms for the purpose of hunting.

10. Guns will be seen mostly on display in history museums with the pictures of the victims of gun violence.

11. The US will stop selling arms, explosives and ammunition to any foreign country and lobby the

international community to sign a non-proliferation treaty.

12. Generally, private citizens will not be allowed to possess firearms.

You may be thinking Basic Common Sense as "radical" and "unrealistic". Maybe we should flip logic on its head and continue doing what doesn't work, because continuing to do what doesn't work and expecting better results is no longer called insanity. It's now called "pragmatic". Yeah, you can now call me an extremist because as George Carlin, the comedian, said I am using **"basic common sense"**.

No one can defend themselves from someone who has a gun and they have the drop on them either at a distance with a rifle or up close with a handgun. You either negotiate or die. I wish weapons for killing humans were never invented but it would be a wasted wish. Many have profited from the manufacture and sale of armaments like Alfred Nobel had done. Other than the practical use of explosives in building things, there is nothing but blood on the hands of these profiteers and manufacturers. I cannot fathom how we give such companies, a license to manufacture items to kill people. Humans are philosophically flawed and prone to fear and negative self deception. Let us not make it legal, easy or even possible for them to purchase weapons of mass killing.

This problem is all about money since nothing else makes sense....

Immortals, the ones prayed to, never wielded a gun or any other weapon for that matter. They were exemplified as loving, peaceful, wise and pure. Immoralists are the ultimate pacifists and would never entertain taking their own lives or anyone else's life. Immortal life is all about living.

Is not death a certainty?

No, it does not have to be a part of living. Death is caused by the ignorance of how to live forever. There was a time when people thought flying from one place to another was impossible. Birds and insects are born with the ability to fly and so were humans. We just had to figure out a way to do it. Just because we are programmed from birth with deathist philosophy does not make it impossible to live forever in the same physical body we started out with at birth.

What do you have to do to collect on your own life insurance policy?

This question is very easy to answer but not simple to do. Just live to be at least a one hundred years old. Whole life policies pay out at that age. Life insurance companies figure you will never make it to 100 and if you do the policy cashes out. It is more of a bookkeeping thing than an incentive to live that long. Term life insurance is unavailable after 70 from most insurance companies.

Living the immortal life physically, mentally and spiritually should take you well beyond the century mark. My first book titled **"How you live one day after forever"** is the blueprint for immortal health. A simple plan but not easy to do in a world dominated by mortals. A world full of dangers administered by thoughtless mortals and owned by greedy corporations.

We, as a society, do not know the secrets of immortal living. We make no effort to discover them and cast our fate to someone else to give us a number based on insurance tables. We even place a bet on how long we will live with life insurance companies and double down on the odds it will be an accident. The older we get the higher the bet (premium) we need to place to insure our death. An insane bet that you will never collect on. Insurance is for the survivors and in a deathist world, which is a good thing to have if you have dependents.

We all know the definition of insanity is doing the same thing over and over and expecting different results. Being born, living a relatively short life and then dying is the deathist's insane behavior. Why not take the alternative approach of immortal living? If you are a believer in reincarnation, why put yourself through childhood reprogramming over and over again. You have survived it once with all of its tribulations; so there is no compelling reason to do it again.

How do you cope with living longer than your mortal relatives and friends?

I have surveyed hundreds of people asking them if they could live in good health forever would they want to live that long. I have re-phased the relative same question by asking them what ripe old age would they like to live to. The answers surprised me. A high percentage stated they would like to live forever to the first question. The second question people answered with a number between 75-80 years. The reasons given for their responses only varied slightly from one person to the next. Essentially they stated that they did not want to outlive their relatives (mostly children) and/or friends.

Of course I had to ask why they felt that way. Believe it or not it had nothing to do with running out of money or becoming infirm. The number one answer was the fear of living longer than someone they cared about. Why did they fear living longer than them? It was a simple fear everyone seems to harbor. The fear of being or dying alone was it.

Why would you not tell your friends or relatives the secret of living forever? If they lived forever like you, would not you like to keep living with them? They seemed to warm to the idea of immortality when they could keep relationships alive forever.

How is death avoidable but not taxes?

A society, like and individual, needs money to survive and function. As a member of society, a community and the world you have the responsibility to fund the commons. It should not be voluntary but required; thus a tax. Avoiding taxes is not just wrong but also irresponsible. It shows disrespect for the government and your neighbors. You may disagree on how tax money is spent and it is your privilege to voice an opinion. Taxes go into a large pot that funds everything society needs to function. As a citizen you have a monetary as well as a community service commitment obligation to fulfill. Utopian government is advanced citizenship and as such requires the participation of all citizens based upon their abilities to contribute. How much and from what sources tax money comes from is decided by the TOIL (Tree of Immortal Living) branch. (more later about the TOIL concept)

What is positive self-deception?

Affirming to yourself something that you can do something difficult, complex or impossible. A type of self-motivation technique wherein you trick yourself into believing something abstract or contrary to popular opinion. It is "I think I can" so will act and believe I can affirmation. It is used to obtain goals, invent things, heal with prayer and overcome the impossible. A mind trick used to persuade your brain to act positive verses negative in relation to a problem. It is looking at situations, relationships or faults with a positive slant. Similar to saying today is going to be better than yesterday or god will save me from the flood.

One powerful way to change any type of behavior pattern is to use the psychological mind trick known as self-deception. Those unfamiliar with this psychological tool; it has been used by us all at one time or another.

Here is how it works. You tell yourself something you want to be true and you act accordingly. Let us say for example you want to the love the pretty girl next door. You tell yourself that she is attracted to you and stare at her as she comes and goes from her house. Although you may never approached her with your admiration you believe she will and does love you. From someone else's perspective you are totally deceiving yourself as to the reality of the situation. In your mind you are making wedding plans. If you explained the way you are thinking and acting to a third party they would think you were dreaming. They would be technically incorrect. Because what you are involved in is self-deception. The reason being is that in addition to thinking your in love with her (dreaming) you are acting as if you are in love with her. The two actions in concert make self-deception.

Acting on your desires creates a motivating force toward a goal. In the above example, if you ask the girl next door to go out on a date you have moved in the direction of marrying the girl. Here comes the self-deception part when you jump from loving her to wanting to possess her in marriage. Not an illogical jump in the relationship in your mind.

Now comes a series of actions towards your goal. You change your behavior so the girl next door notices you. Then you invest in yourself to make yourself more appealing. You may buy new clothes or an attractive car or maybe start working out to enhance your physical appearance. You are in love with an idea. Whether it becomes a reality or not you are telling yourself it is real and doing your best to make it happen. Self-deception has spawned self-motivation. Your actions become focused on gaining the love of the girl next door.

Is this a bad thing? Not really, people need self-guidance. It is a part of that precious gift known as "free will". When you believe in anything that you cannot objectively prove to be true or real, you are practicing self-deception. Sounds kind of negative when summarized in those words. Especially when the word believe is attached to any abstract phenomenon. Believe me that this is true. Okay that was uncalled for. But believe me when I say all beliefs are self-deceptions until they become facts.

Remember when I stated previously that self-deception was a powerful tool. It is a fact. There are two types of self-deception. Positive wherein the behavior of the individual results in or leads to growth and enlightenment. Such things as prosperity, good fortune, or a feeling of accomplishment are positive self-deception. Like actually having the girl next door falling in love with you and living together in total happiness. Your positive self-deception became a reality. You started out believing it was possible and it became a fact. Professional athletes start out with a positive self-deception to become what they achieve. Another name for it is believing in themselves.

What is negative self-deception?

Negative self-deception is very destructive and depressing. When you tell yourself it not possible to do something before you even try to achieve it. You say to yourself the girl next door would never love me, I don't believe in true love and marriage seldom works out well. No dream and no action, just depression is the result.

Depression is a huge worldwide problem mistakenly treated with pharmaceuticals in most cases. It is a philosophical problem that should be treated with strong motivational leadership, positive self-deception and compassion.

There is the more destructive form of self-deception called negative self-deception wherein the individual seeks a negative result. The criminal minded or the greedy run amok are examples of the destructive force of negative self-deception.

Here a person seizes on the idea of conning a group of people out of their money by plotting a scheme in their mind (the dream). They then contact the people with a phishing email to get banking information, passwords and identity facts (action). They then use the information to access their money and credit. They then, without remorse, spend the money on themselves feeling all the time like they earned it. The more they do this type of negative behavior the greater the motivation for greed gets for them. Eventually guilt or the life style will destroy them. Going to prison does not break the cycle of negative self-deception. It tends to reinforce it by introducing the individual to other people with the same mind set (negative self-deception reinforcement). Prison only becomes a time out if real rehabilitation is not applied to the individual's mental problem. This is why the cycle of crime (recidivism) is rarely effectively dealt with by incarnation alone. Intervention must take place to create a positive self-deception. One of the worst things society does is branding a criminal with a record and denying the individual access to positive employment opportunities. This type of life long punishment after punishment is neither a deterrent to future crime or a way to warn the general public of a possible threat. Branding is only effective on livestock and there are ways around that kind of branding by rustlers.

Why wouldn't alcohol, drugs or tobacco be a problem in an immortalist society?

Alcohol, drugs and tobacco products are not something a true immortalist would partake in. All three categories are toxic to the human body and destroy the lives of the users thereof. Like guns societies are awash in both legal and illegal drugs all of which kill humans before and after maturity. Again, the driving force behind the proliferation is greed and monied interests. Everyone knows they cause social, physiological and psychological problems for the users of each of these substances. A thinking person would not indulge in any of them. Any attempt to make them illegal would fail as it has for most of history. Education and a strong opposing philosophy like immortalism is the only way to diminish the negative influence they have on society. The only viable way to deal with abuse is rehabilitation. Imprisonment is not an effective deterrent and only amplifies problem and costs far more capital than rehabilitation. Establishments that cater to the these human weaknesses have no place in an immortalist world. I know this kind of discipline is a deal breaker for the social drinkers in the world; but they will get over it.

"Only two things are infinite, the universe and human stupidity, and I'm not sure about the former." Albert Einstein

How would immortals deal with crime?

It would be naive to think that even a society governed by immortalist created laws and principles would be crime free. However, handling the way such individuals are incarcerated and rehabilitated would be significantly different.

Every crime is committed by either an individual with a long term negative self-deception or a short term emotional lapse of judgement. This creates two classifications of criminals. Of course it could be an individual is classified as both types. In that case, both types of treatment would need to be applied. Instead of the traditional method of the punishment must fit the crime, the immortalist approach would be the individual fits the punishment (rehabilitation).

There are two generic existing classifications of criminals; violent and non-violent. Although this serves a purpose in segregating prisoners it does nothing to facilitate rehabilitation.

A person found guilty or confesses to a crime has a negative self-deception or an emotional self-control issue; maybe both. The person needs reprogramming, compassion, redemption, recycling, and a way to atone for their crime(s). There is a very large range of criminal behavior to deal with using any set approach. Doing a one size fits all approach is just plain being lazy and simplistic. So much depends on the individual and the circumstances surrounding the commission of the crime.

Fear of punishment is not an effective deterrent to the commission of most crime. Like a lock on a door is no obstacle to a person wanting to trespass. It is only there to keep out an honest person.   Humans are basically good, peaceful, warm and capable of loving themselves and others. It is when competition, stress, despair and a sense wrongful entitlement takes over their internal and/or external environment that they deviate from their natural order. Much like the physical world, when chaos is introduced into the normal mind the effect causes irrational behavior. Remove the cause of the chaos and the mind returns to a rational behavior pattern.

Of course, I invite many critics of this approach to criminals and their behavior. Revenge is a powerful emotion when an individual is a victim of a criminal act. We feel violated and insecure. There is little to no forgiveness for the perpetrators. Typical reaction is to do as much as possible to prevent being a victim a second time. Many victims increase physical security and want law enforcement to remove the perpetrators predominately from their environment. A lock them up and throw away the key mentality.... Revenge!

This does not fix the problem, it creates a whole set of expensive new problems. You are merely dealing with the effect of the crime and not the cause. You must realize crime is irrational behavior that needs remedial action to eliminate the cause. The criminal is a broken person that needs repairs. Punishing a criminal without removing the cause of their behavior only makes them motivated not to get caught the next time. It does not address the issue of why the crime was committed in the first place.

An immortalist system of justice would be totally different from the systems we are familiar with today. Police would have no lethal weapons and would be trained and equipped to subdue an individual. Criminals using or possessing, with intent, lethal weapons to threaten or murder other humans have given up their right to life.

Now, you would deduce that the only way to deal with gun toting violent individuals or similar type of threats from armed aggression would be with lethal force. The use of military like tactics by police. Well, this is how society has dealt with these situations for all of its history. Wars, terrorist attacks, power grabs and all types of feuds. Whenever someone or a group of someones is attacked we counter attack. Revenge is rearing its ugly head which only leads to more death.

As a civilization, government or individual we have learned nothing from thousands of years of violence and wars. By meeting aggression with aggression, force with force, violence with violence, and death with revenge the cycle of death by lethal force continues. What has society learned from all of this maiming and killing? Virtually nothing!

Addressing a problem of this magnitude over and over again with force and revenge has been pure insanity. The result has been the same each and every time. We increase our security measures, arm ourselves more and continue to live in fear.

What is the greatest obstacle to living an immortal life?

Ask this question to any mortal and they would say it would be "death". A mortal believes death seems to be a certainty. Mortals are missing the point of immortalist philosophy. It is not about not dying. It is about "living". Living like you are not going to die. You are putting death out of your mindset. If you think about it, you do not plan your day around dying. In fact most people do not think they are going to die any day; just sometime in the distant future. So living like you are not going to die each day is natural. Congratulations, you already know how to think and live like an immortal. Now all you need to do is live.

As the technology of warfare has advanced to weapons of mass destruction, nations have banned together to control the use and proliferation. A line in the sand has been drawn to keep them out of the hands of mass murders. However, once the Genie is out of the bottle, so to speak, it is near impossible to put back in. It is only a matter of time until a failed state uses biological, chemical or nuclear weapons against a perceived enemy to exact revenge.

What does this all mean to the immortalist? Besides being an end of life issue for them, this is a major problem for them to solve as quickly as possible. How do you disarm the world? When does a person lay down his weapons and remove the locks from his doors and the bars from his windows?

A lesson from the Cold War Era contains a piece of the answer to this difficult question. A phenomenon known as mutual self-destruction caused nations to restrain themselves from initiating war on each other. The philosophy at play here is no one wants to fight a battle they have no chance of winning unless they are suicidal. It was the philosophy supported by the facts that prevented irrational behavior. So the only thing that will make a person lay down their arms and unlock their doors is a philosophy that makes them believe they cannot seek either revenge or destruction without losing the things they should want most of all: Life, liberty, security, peace and happiness. Life is the number one item on the list.

What is this philosophy? The philosophy is immortalism. Given a person truly understands they only have one life to live, that there is no life after death, or a heaven not on earth, or reincarnation and that they can live forever in the body they were born with; then and only then, can that person learn to get along with everyone and lay down their weapons and unlock their doors. It is then, no rational reason to want to die or risk imprisonment will exist.

This philosophy has been working on a large scale of the world population for many centuries without people thinking about it. It works in limited fashion each and every day. We call it law and order or peaceful coexistence. A majority of the world's people have no weapons and do leave their doors unlocked; if they have doors. These people do not let fears change or rule their lives. They realize the futility of trying to prevent something that may never happen and that locks and guns only makes their lives more difficult and expensive. They understand the axiom that only a fearful person can be sold a burglar alarm.

Can you have a society without fear?

It will be difficult to totally eliminate fear and fear mongering. It is deeply entrenched in our cultures. Frightening people is a political, salesmanship and theatrical art form. The one thing we, as a society, cannot allow is for fear to dominate our lives.

Society needs to relax, chill out, and act fearless in a rational way.

One person told me the reason they don't lock their doors is because "they did want to have someone need to be breaking in". Another stated "they did not want to be prisoners in their own home". Here are some other rational statements about why people do not want locks and other security measures.

"Walls and locks keep people out but they also keep people in."

"What if I had to leave in a hurry because of a fire or something."

" How can I watch out for my neighbor if I cannot see beyond the fence."

"People around here respect other people's properties and privacy."

"People will knock, call out or ring the bell if they want to see us or come in."

What about strangers? "They know the rules of politeness and most follow them."

"I welcome people to my home who want to visit. I don't lock them inside when they come calling."

"If the law needs to search my home, for probable cause, then they do not need to break down my door."

"A salesman going door to door is only doing his job and trying to make a living for himself and his family. He will knock if he wants my business. If I am busy or not interested he will politely leave."

"I used to lock and bolt my doors until one day I needed help and people could not get in the door. I don't lock the bathroom door anymore for the same reason."

"I prefer to yell "come on in" rather than answer the door all the time."

"When I work in the store the door is always open and strangers come and go all day without causing me no harm. There is even money in the cash register. Why should I worry about strangers coming to my home where there isn't much worth taking."

"Fear is for fools who think they can stop a train by standing on the tracks."

"Security is an illusion created by lock, alarm and gun sellers."

"I have insurance on my stuff so if someone wants it bad enough to steal it then let them have it. I can always buy a new one."

"I dug a moat around my house and filled it with water and alligators. The alligators crawled out and tried to eat me. So I got a gun and killed all the gators. I drained the moat because the mosquitos came and began stinging me. A child fell into the moat hole and the parents sued me. They won a judgement against me and I had to sell my house to pay it. Now I am homeless and have no doors to lock. I no longer fear someone might enter the flap on the cardboard box I now live inside."

"The door to heaven or hell is always open so who am I to close mine."

"The church down the street locks its doors at night to keep the sinners out. Now isn't that ironic."

"Only prisons and jails need to have locks and alarms because those people want to be free. I am free and want to feel that way."

"I have a small garden where I grow vegetables and flowers. I put my surplus out by the road with a can for money. People stop, pay what they think is fair in the can. Sometimes they even make change from the can. No one steals the money or the produce. Why? I guess people are essentially honest and grateful."

"If someone comes to my door asking for food or water, I graciously give it to them. To deny it to them forces them to steal to survive. Survival is instinctive behavior and so is kindness or charity." *

We already have a portion of society without irrational fear. All we have to do is cultivate those seeds and grow them in minds of the fearful.

* *Survey was taken in a large metropolitan area.*

How to deal with drugs, alcohol, tobacco and other such substances?

It would be naive to count on a change in philosophy eliminating the use and sale of harmful drugs, alcohol products, tobacco and other known harmful substances. The addictive nature of these items and the wide usage of them in the world preclude humans going cold turkey. Some cultures even include them in their religious ceremonies; although not in an abusive manner. The question is how to regulate the sale and use of these known to be harmful substances.

Education is one approach which may curtail some usage. Placing warning labels on the products which detail the side-effects and safety hazards are not very effective. Regulating the environment where sellers and users can congregate and partake safely and responsibly is a rational way to minimize the potential impact on non-users. Making the substances illegal has proven to be totally ineffective and only creates criminals and blackmarkets. Taxing only creates blackmarkets and encourages unlicensed manufacturers who may produce dangerous substitutes. People must be held criminally liable for any acts while under the influence and placed in rehabilitation. Reducing users is the only viable method of controlling abuse and criminal behavior.

What about property rights and privacy in a immortalist society?

Property rights and privacy is an illusion created by some governments to protect officials and businesses from intelligent oversight. People actually think these rights extend to them in a modern society. These rights are abridged, at the slightest provocation and often, without due process under any laws.

In an immortalist society there are limited property rights. A person has the right to responsibly utilize property they have earned the privilege to utilize.

For example a person leases a taxi with money they have earned by working a job. The taxi is under their exclusive control for the purpose of transporting themselves and others following the rules and regulations of operating such a vehicle on public roads for profit or convenience. The care, insurance and maintenance of the taxi is responsibility of the user(s) of the taxi under the terms set forth by the manufacturer who provides the servicing of the taxi. The lessee of the taxi may transfer the lease to another party for the same purpose for a monetary consideration. If the taxi is destroyed or economically unrepairable for some reason the lease is over, the taxi is recycled, and they may lease another one at market price. Notice that there was no mention of a bank or credit company in this example. The lessee (may be a group of individuals) must purchase the lease upfront. The manufacturer, owned by the employees, gets the startup funding solely from the government, upon application, which must be repaid within a set period. Employees have an interest in the taxi (product) and the assets of the manufacturer. This example shows the little difference between responsible use of a taxi and the ownership of a taxi. Not much difference between the two but a lot of difference in how the taxi is operated and manufactured and what happens to it once its serviceable life is over. There is also a huge difference in way the taxi is manufactured, taking into account environmental issues and consumer safety.

Privacy is a matter of respect for the lives and social customs of others. It is the state or condition of being free from being observed or disturbed by other people. A right is a moral or legal entitlement to have or obtain something or to act in a certain way. The right of privacy is often extended to wear you sleep, go to the bathroom, your personal effects and writings. In a mature society, in a time of peace and tranquillity, this right of privacy is given without reservation. This right is unenforceable when a society is under duress. You can expect it but never count on it.

How do immortals deal with poverty and world hunger?

Poverty and world hunger are related to several factors. Chiefly, it is the product of corporate greed and poor management of agricultural lands by government entities. Of course, overpopulation and climate related events play a large part in the mix.

Poverty tends to be generational and difficult to break free from without the benefit of a good education. Often exploitation by corporate employers who fail to pay a livable wage leads to virtual enslavement of workers. Faced with unemployment and starvation workers submit to an economic environment difficult to break away from. Add to this a tendency to produce more offspring than they can support and the shortened lifespans of the male parent, you have the spiral of poverty.

Immortals, in control of society, would ensure employers pay a livable wage, provide free education to all citizens, impose health and safety standards to protect workers, encourage planned parenthood and make housing more affordable for working families. Sounds reasonable and there should be no reason other than greed and a society that thinks poverty is wholly self-inflicted and a matter of choice. None chooses to be poor and hungry. It is the economic environment that creates this phenomenon. An environment that these unfortunate people have no control over. Society does have or should have control over this environment. Even if it is impossible to fix in their particular location, society should relocate them to a more favorable geographical location. It is far more logical to relocate a population than to make them refugees who scatter themselves all over the world where they become unwanted and discriminated against.

Is there immortals living amongst us?

Yes, there are even groups and organizations in the world you can become a member of. My upcoming book titled "Who is 1251?" is about a person claiming to be an immortal.

What is deathist philosophy?

Deathist philosophy is the belief that everything lives and ultimately dies. A philosophy enforced from early childhood development through the observation of death of animals, death of family members, video, movies, signs of aging, religious teaching, games, literature and observation.

A negative self-deception which causes mortals to participate in risky behavior, war, drugs and causes high rates of cancer and other diseases. The deathist philosophy is the leading cause of depression among old and young people. If you believe your going die or ultimately will die is deathist thinking. People actually **do will** themselves to die.

The Deathist Philosophy is the major impediment to persuading someone to change how they view life and the world around them. An alternate term would be to call it mortalist philosophy and would academically be more correct way of stating the opposite philosophy to immortalist philosophy. However, it confuses the issue when two words sound similar and there meanings are totally opposite of each other. So I coined the term **'Deathist Philosophy'**. Besides contrasting the two ways of thinking, deathist has a negative cogitation to it that I like to imprint on people.

A deathist has been programmed to think that life is finite and maybe cheap. Living is and dying is the natural cycle of life. Everyone has told them it is so and demonstrated it to them in countless ways. No one has ever shown them anything to the contrary. They believe it and then, without question, turn around and worship immortals. They even go all in on the idea of immortal life after death; although they have no proof of it. A deathist is often suicidal because of this one belief of life after death. **They live their entire life dedicated to the idea of life after death being better than being alive**. They invent ways to die and kill others all the while worshipping their immortal god(s). You may think, I think this is stupid behavior. I do not think it is stupid given how a deathist is taught about life.

A deathist has little choice in the matter. A deathist is blinded to the facts and ignorant of how to behave otherwise. No one has ever sat him or her down and questioned their deathist philosophy or challenged them to think or act differently. Why? Because everyone they know or interact with has the same philosophy as they do. Besides according to 16th Edition of Bartlett's Familiar Quotations Emily Dickerson wrote: *"The only secret people keep Is Immortality"*. What a shame to keep immortality a secret! I always have stated there are too many secrets in this world. Maybe it is like the famous line Jack Nicholson, the actor, recited from the movie: A Few Good Men *"You can't handle the truth"*!

Deathist can have a problem facing the possibility of immortality. It is a truth they are unprepared to deal with on several levels. It would upset their view of the world and their place in it. One person remarked to me if immortality meant that they would have to walk around in white robes with their hands folded all the time. I laughed and told them that was just the thought a religious person would have about being an immortal. The ideal outfit for a saint or a godlike figure. A great outfit to set them apart from the deathists but they were missing the point.

The point being is that no one is watching you from above so to speak. You are the person in charge of your life, not some supreme being with a secret plan for you. Assuming you are an adult, how you live is your choice. Remember the free will clause in your spiritual contract with your god. Also, you are the one that chooses to die. Yes, you choose to die. The manner of death you may also choose but most of us leave it up to fate. At least that is what we tell ourselves during the short time we live. We spend our lives like we are on a short trip through time lasting less than 100 years. Everyone wants to live to be a hundred but less than 1% actually do. Why?

When the game is over the king and the pawn go in the same box. - A Chess Game metaphor for life and death.

Did God make us immortals?

So if you believe in the words written in the several versions of the bible, the answer is yes. The passage essentially states we were made in his image. Since God is an immortal being, so it follows we are also immortal.

Then God said, "Let Us make man in Our image, according to Our likeness; and let them rule over the fish of the sea and over the birds of the sky and over the cattle and over all the earth, and over every creeping thing that creeps on the earth." God created man in His own image, in the image of God He created him; male and female He created them. God blessed them; and God said to them, "Be fruitful and multiply, and fill the earth, and subdue it; and rule over the fish of the sea and over the birds of the sky and over every living thing that moves on the earth."...
Genesis 1:27

Is immortality a result of evolution or intelligent design?

Both evolution and intelligent design are at play. An entity made the human form. Design necessitates a designer. This is a fundamental axiom. When we apply the general principles of detecting specified complexity to living creatures, we find it reasonable to infer the presence of intelligent design. Common sense demands a Designer. In general, we find "specified complexity" to be a reliable indicator of the presence of intelligent design. Chance can explain complexity but not specification; a random sequence of letters is complex but not specified (it is meaningless). A Bob Dylan song is both complex and specified (it is meaningful).
You can't have a Bob Dylan song without Bob Dylan.

Living creatures do tend to evolve and the human form has evolved through the millenniums. It is not absurd to deduce that a designer may have made a few prototypes before making the current human form as we know it. So Darwin's evolution theory may be correct that we descended from the design of apes. A few design changes to apes and presto you have man.

If we all started living forever, would we need a bigger planet?

A valid concern, since the world population is already 7 billion and counting. Over population is a serious threat to the survival of humanity and the environment. Disease, war, genocide, starvation and birth control is not enough to curb population growth. Also, anything other than birth control is a horrific alternative method of controlling the population. Travel to distant earth like planets is far in the future for the general public and probably not a valid solution for survival on earth.

Again, we must institute a new philosophy to control the human urge to reproduce. The philosophy is immortalism because it is the one philosophy that can automatically curtail the urge to reproduce. Once society is convinced that they can live forever in the bodies they were born with, there is no urge to reproduce to insure the survival of the species. An infinite lifespan that is only curtailed by chance and suicide lends itself to planned parenthood. This means only reproduction to replace or no reproduction at all would occur in society. Deathist would find it hard to believe this is possible.

Deathists have become accustomed to forming families via marriage. A couple comes together for the purpose of fostering children. The children mature and marry and produce more offspring within a thirty year period. They in turn marry and produce offspring. All this happens within the current lifespan of the great grandparents. Now two people have produced sixteen or more offspring only if each generation had two offspring per marriage. Even a one child rule per couple only slows down population growth.

It is a proven fact that well educated, productive and creative members of a society do not reproduce like the polar opposites in society, who tend to overproduce offspring. Immoralists would fit into the first group of non-producers of high amounts of offspring. Given to the knowledge of the dangers of overpopulation to a society and you have, at a minimum, zero population growth.

The key to the success of this immortalist theory of population control is education and a significant reduction in the factors that cause the urge to reproduce in geographical locations prone to war, starvation, exploitation and religious dogma. It is not enough to suspend the influence of these factors causing females to reproduce. They must become so extinct as to make the influence a distant memory. A total emersion into a new philosophical society lacking those negative factors is the only viable solution.

Now I am going to state some things that will not sit well with deathists. Artificial insemination needs to be banned until every orphan in the world is adopted. Adoption by childless couples should be subsidized by the government and free with qualification. Also, birth control items need to be subsidized and readily available to all citizens. Religious organizations and government agencies need to encourage or not resist birth control. Global warming and climate change is directly related to human overpopulation. Humans must understand the impact that one has upon the other. Abortion needs to be safe, free and legal everywhere. Producing offspring should require prior approval and qualification. The health and financial profiles of the parents must be considered. Parenting is an awesome and longterm responsibility. We, as a society, have left it up to fate and the untrained for thousands of years. Now at seven billion and counting, it is time to change this insane practice of producing human offspring with no planning or control. Birthing is not a human right; it is a human responsibility that must be taken seriously. Marry whomever you love. Have sex as much as you want but do not create children that are not wanted or planned.

"In my next life I want to live my life backwards. You start out dead and get that out of the way. Then you wake up in an old people's home feeling better every day. You get kicked out for being too healthy, go collect your pension, and then when you start work, you get a gold watch and a party on your first day. You work for 40 years until you're young enough to enjoy your retirement. You party, drink alcohol, and are generally promiscuous, then you are ready for high school. You then go to primary school, you become a kid, you play. You have no responsibilities, you become a baby until you are born. And then you spend your last 9 months floating in luxurious spa-like conditions with central heating and room service on tap, larger quarters every day and then Voila! You finish off as an orgasm!"
— Woody Allen

⊕Chapter 5

Immortal Structure

What guidance is important for a Immortalist Society?

#1 Respect in Society

Overall Guidance Statement

"Respect for all living things, other humans, the environment, and the universe we live in."

A. Respect for all humans without a trace of bigotry, discrimination or regard to physical ability.

B. Respect for all domesticated and wild animals and their habitats. All hunting and animal farming techniques strictly regulated or prohibited.

C. Respect for authority and the principles, laws and regulations they have been sworn to enforce with compassion, tolerance, professionalism, and integrity.

D. Respect for the laws of nature, science, ethnic traditions and historical properties.

E. Respect for public and private property open to use by all humans.

F. Respect for workers, employers, safety rules, and the working environment. All people capable of work should be employed in some manner in accordance with their abilities at a wage sufficient to insure their basic needs in the society they reside.

Respect is the key to the success of a family, community, a state, a country, a nation, a continent, the world, the planet and the universe. It cannot be circumvented, conditional, or abridged by authority, civil disobedience or religious dogma. It is without question, the most important thing needed to be taught to impressionable children and young adults. Respect also needs to be woven into the discourse to all people and in society of all ages. Highlighting and exemplifying respect should be the day to day norm of the leadership, the media and the educational system. Disrespect should be admonished at every opportunity as an example of what is not acceptable behavior. Under no circumstances should disrespect be codified into our culture, arts or social media.

Parents or those responsible for parenting are the ones who need to be the prime force behind the teaching of respect and the ones who must set the examples. It starts with the parents showing great respect for each other. It flows from there to how the parents react to the people, related or non-related to them, in everyday conversation and interaction. Parents must be durable and unrelenting examples of respectful behavior.

The most durable and successful societies to date were built on the principles and foundation of respectful behavior. They were referred to as "polite societies" and became strong influences in the world. Unfortunately, their influence has wained over time as greed and unbridled power has destroyed the credibility and reputation they projected. Most waged class warfare, thus a societal wedge or division occurred as a result.

Greed further eroded their position as an example of acceptable behavior. When a society excludes or diminishes members of their population a society losses mutual respect for each other. The perception of the excluded class is one of envy and disgust. All respect is lost and may become totally unrecoverable. As the distance between the haves and have nots widens. Lawlessness becomes epidemic. Blackmarkets, organized crime, gang warfare and corruption in government take hold. Ultimately, if allowed to fester, downgrades into civil war or revolution.

#2 Trust

"Trust is the firm belief in the reliability, truth, ability or strength of someone or something."

A. Trust in yourself, your family and your neighbor to do the right thing no matter the consequences.
B. Trust your government to act in the best interests of all the citizenry when establishing laws and regulations.

C. Trust scientific facts and what you see with your own eyes in person.
D. Trust in safety devices and use them in your daily life.
E. Earn other peoples trust with consistent positive attitude and honesty.
F. Trust the strength and design of your body to heal itself and live on.

Without trust there is no viable relationship with anyone or any entity. If you do not trust your spouse your marriage is doomed to failure. Trusting your neighbor or fellow citizen is how the world needs to work. We all trust that the sun will come up tomorrow. We plan our lives on trust. We trust that if we do our jobs we will be rewarded with money or credit. We place our trust in our public safety officers, the firefighters, the paramedics and other first responders will come when we need them. We trust other people to do their jobs with respect and efficiency.

#3 Safety

"Safety is the condition of being protected from or unlikely to cause danger, risk or injury."

A. Safety is everyone's responsibility to follow and maintain.
B. Safety needs to be learned and applied to all aspects of living.
C. Safety training must be given to each employee by their employer.
D. Safety engineering is a high priority profession in an immortal's society.
E. Safe water, safe food, safe air and a safe place to lay or heads at night.

Air & Water

Polluting the air we all breath or the water we drink should be criminalized in every corner of the world. All profit from doing so, confiscated. All witting persons jailed and their property confiscated by the world court. All major cases adjudicated within 90 days and assets frozen until judgement is rendered. Minor cases within 30 days. Any corporation found guilty of such crimes will be dissolved and the assets confiscated by the court. No fines will be allowed in lieu corporate death. All officers, of a convicted corporation, will at a minimum, have their personal assets confiscated and will be imprisoned with mandatory sentences. The court will determine which officers and board members were involved.

The stock holders will lose all value to the court for wittingly or unwittingly funding a polluter. Any bank or other financial institution will lose all interest in the assets of a convicted polluter to the court. The court will auction the assets and apply all proceeds to the clean-up of the environment or enforcement of strict environmental laws. No person, government, religious organization, or business entity will be allowed to pollute the environment without a method of filtering out 90 percent of all harmful substances and balancing out or containing the effects of the remaining 10 percent on human health. All mass energy production must be by renewable sources. Individual use of fossil fuels in primitive areas will be tolerated for energy production only. Open fires will be restricted. Primitive areas to be defined as geographical locations without wired telecommunication service and basic utilities such as electricity, water, or sewage.

Burning of refuse and crop land cover or waste will be prohibited. All human produced waste must be recycled. Water, land, space and air pollution are to be internationally regulated and uniformly applied regardless of any other governmental laws or permits. No loopholes, no exception and zero tolerance. Pollution laws and environmental care must be a mandatory part of all world educational and informational systems.

Ask yourself, is it in your best interests to support such a radical approach. If your answer is maybe then you are halfway towards being concerned about your health. If it is yes you understand what is at risk. If your answer is no, read no further, you are not concerned with your health, your children's health, or anyone else's welfare including your own. Good luck because that is all you have going for you. Immortals understand the importance of pure water and clean air.

Food Safety

Whether it is chemical safety, dietary supplements, cosmetics, genetic engineering, nutrition labeling, antimicrobial resistance, review of animal drugs, or ensuring that we have the right technologies to identify hazards in the commodities we consume, all of these issues will impact the public health.

A public health agency first and foremost is where our focus should be, using the core principle of science and tools such as regulation, guidance, research, outreach and education to get us there.

Food safety is extremely important to immortals. All citizens and students need comprehensive education in the proper storage, preparation, harvesting and processing of food. The farming of, transportation of and the marketing of food items needs to be highly regulated and transparent. There should be more health inspectors than police officers in populated areas.

All food and menu items need to include information on sourcing, nutrition, toxicity and digestibility How we fuel our bodies is the key to immortal physical health and longevity.

What are the governmental priorities of an immortocracy?

Humans require eleven basic items to live stress free in society:

- Potable Water for drinking and bathing
- Clean Air to breath
- Sanitary facilities for human waste
- Systems to collect and transport in conjunction with facilities to recycle man made materials
- Shelter in accordance with the environment
- Safe food to maintain optimum health

- Trauma Care when required
- Safety of your person and private property
- Access to knowledge and information
- A method to communicate with other humans
- Some type of Employment or Service Opportunity

1. Construct and maintain potable water and sewage treatment systems within its territorial boundaries for the use of all life forms in a manner not harmful to the environment or ecological systems. Power generation and energy systems using renewable resources under the same guidelines.

2. Construct and maintain public roads, mass transit systems, railway systems, public schools and universities, libraries and achieves, shelters for displaced individuals and the general population in preparation for natural disasters within its territorial boundaries for the use of all life forms in a manner not harmful to the environment or ecological systems.

3. Establish and maintain Public Safety systems for the general population involving the participation general population in the systems daily operation without the use of firearms or other forms of lethal force. All able bodied

citizens need to trained to perform Public Safety duties under the supervision of a permanent sworn officer. Public Safety courses should a part of primary and secondary school curriculum.

4. Establish and maintain First Responder Units and   Care Centers for fire, traumas, accidents and natural disasters. Manned by core professionals and augmented by trained volunteers.

These items may seem simplistic but life and living was never meant to be a struggle. Keeping things simple is the key to a stressless life.   Stress is a killer. Complexity creates jobs but also compounds the problems for leadership and society as a whole.

🍒Chapter 6

We the Immortal People

Why does an immortocracy need a Constitution?

A Constitution is a blueprint for any society; especially a new one. In order to build anything complex and substantial you need a plan. A plan that is more than a scribbling on a cocktail napkin. It is one thing to profess an idea or philosophical theory but another to actually build it. A constitution is the specifications of how that idea is to be constructed and maintained. It is a boundary document used to keep a society from straying away from the principles it was founded on. The better the boundaries are clearly defined the easier it will keep society from contorting it.

I took the constitutions of two relatively successful countries, The Peoples Republic of China and the United States of America and took what I thought were the best parts. I added in the immortalist philosophy and fixed what, I thought, was problematic for each country throughout their respective constitutional histories. I also analyzed the good and the bad of all the other "isms" and dictatorships. I eliminated politics, direct elections of representatives, heads of state and private ownership of the commons and land.

The U.S. two party political system is wrought with endless investigations, taxpayer-funded witch hunts, complete obstruction of any major legislation and special interest influence. The Chinese political system produces major economies with high growth rates of state investment (China, India) have high rates of economic growth. The major economies with low growth rates of state investment, such as the U.S. and Europe, have low rates of economic growth. It is clearly Socialism vs Corporatism wherein the socialist state takes its profits and reinvests it in the people's needs and in the corporate state the profits go to the richest one percent and no further. China's main fault is not instituting a minimum wage and letting foreign companies exploit its labor force and environment.

The constitution is of **'The People's Elysian Existence'**. Elysian is another word for heavenly, paradisal, paradisiacal, celestial or divine. Existence is a state of living, having objective reality or continued survival. Together it is the people's heavenly continued survival. A fitting name for what this constitution is designed to create. It may be a dream but sometimes dreams do become true; with a little help from everyone and an immortal or two.

Life was never meant to be a struggle. Life on Earth can be heaven, which the grand designer intended it to be. The beauty and splendor of this planet is here for us all to learn to enjoy. You have been given this opportunity through the miracle of birth; so don't squander it. Live intelligently without fear or abandon.

National Anthem of The People's Elysian Existence by:

Matteo Marini & Ellie Lawson - Dreaming Of A Better World

There is nothing to worry about, there
is nothing to fear
The sun still shines through the rainy
skies and I'll be right here

Even in the darkest moments
Theres always a way
Keep looking for the light that shines
bright
The love in a brand new day

Keep talking about a better world
Keep dreaming about a better world
See it clear keep thinking it out loud
And one day you'll be heard

I'm dreaming of a better world
I'm dreaming of a better world

I'm dreaming of a better world
I'm dreaming of a better world

There is nothing to worry about, there
is nothing to fear
The sun still shines through the rainy
skies and I'll be right here

Theres no right way to live
Theres no right way to be
Keep doing the best you can
And soon you'll see

Keep talking about a better world
Keep dreaming about a better world
See it clear keep thinking it out loud
And one day you'll be heard

Keep talking about a better world
Keep dreaming bout a better world
See it clear keep thinking it out loud
And one day you'll be heard

I'm dreaming of a better world
I'm dreaming of a better world

I'm dreaming of a better world
I'm dreaming of a better world
I'm dreaming of a better world

I'm dreaming of a better world
I'm dreaming of a better world
I'm dreaming of a better world
I'm dreaming of a better world
I'm dreaming of a better world

Available on iTunes

https://itunes.apple.com/us/album/
dreaming-better-world-extended/
id803520485?i=803520496

PREAMBLE

WE THE IMMORTAL PEOPLE OF THE PLANET EARTH, IN ORDER TO FORM A MORE PERFECT WORLD, ESTABLISH JUSTICE, INSURE WORLD TRANQUILITY, INSTILL RESPECT FOR ALL HUMAN AND ANIMAL LIFE, PROMOTE THE GENERAL WELFARE AND SECURE THE

BLESSINGS OF
LIBERTY TO
OURSELVES AND OUR
POSTERITY, DO
ORDAIN AND
ESTABLISH THIS
CONSTITUTION FOR
THE BETTERMENT OF
ALL THE PEOPLE

CONSTITUTION OF THE PEOPLE'S ELYSIAN EXISTENCE

Article 1. Immortalist State

The Immortocracy is an immortalist state under the people's democratic consent led by the Members of all the Branches of the TREE OF IMMORTAL LIVING (TOIL) and based on the alliance of all human genders.
The TOIL system is the basic system of The People's Elysian Existence an Immortocracy. Disruption of the TOIL system by any organization or individual is prohibited.

Article 2. Power Belongs To The People

All power in the Immortocracy belongs to the people.

152

Unions and the local people's caucus at various levels are the organs through which the people input ideas to the various TOILs.
The people administer state affairs and manage economic, cultural and social affairs through various channels and in various ways in accordance with the law.

Article 3. Democracy
The state organs of The People's Elysian Existence apply the principle of democratic centralism.
The TOIL and the local people's caucuses at various levels are constituted through democratic competitions. They are responsible to the people and subject to their supervision. All administrative, judicial and administrative organs of the state are created by the TOIL to which they are responsible and by which they are supervised.
The divisions of functions and powers between the central and local state organs is guided by the principle of giving full scope to the initiative and enthusiasm of the local authorities under the unified leadership of the centralized TOILs.

Article 4. Ethic And Cultural Minority Rights

All nationalities in The People's Elysian Existence are equal. The state protects the lawful rights and interests of the minority nationalities and upholds and develops a relationship of equality, unity and mutual assistance among all of Planet's nationalities. Discrimination against and oppression of any nationality are prohibited; any act which undermines the unity of the nationalities or instigates division is prohibited.

The state assists areas inhabited by a visible minority accelerating their economic and cultural development according to the characteristics and needs of the various visible minorities.

All people have the freedom to use and develop their own spoken and written languages and to preserve or reform their own folkways and customs; however, all people must be literate in the universal language designated by the Media Branch of the TOIL.

Article 5. Judicial Power

The judicial Power of The People's Elysian Existence, shall be vested in one supreme court with the members thereof appointed by the Judicial Branch of the TOIL and in such inferior courts as the TOIL may from time to time ordain and establish. The judges, both of the supreme and inferior courts, shall hold their offices during good behavior, and shall, at stated times, receive for services a compensation which shall not be diminished during their continuance in office.

The judicial power shall extend to all cases, in Law and Equity, arising under this Constitution, the Laws of The People's Elysian Existence, and Treaties made, or which shall be made, under their authority; to all cases affecting Ambassadors, other public Ministers and Consuls; to all cases of admiralty and maritime Jurisdiction; to Controversies to which The People's Elysian Existence shall be a Party. In all Cases affecting Ambassadors, other public Ministers and Consuls, and those in which a State shall be Party, the supreme Court shall have original Jurisdiction. In all the other Cases before mentioned, the supreme Court shall have appellate Jurisdiction, both as to Law and Fact, with such Exceptions, and under such Regulations as the TOIL shall make.

The Trial of all Crimes shall be by Jury; and such Trial shall be held in the area where the said crimes shall have been committed.

Article 6. Constitutional Supremacy

The People's Elysian Existence practices ruling the planet in accordance with the law and building a immortalist society of laws. The immortocracy upholds the uniformity and dignity of the immortalist legal system. No laws or administrative or local rules and regulations may contravene the Constitution. All TOIL Branches, public organizations and all enterprises and institutions must abide by the Constitution and the law. All acts in violation of the Constitution and the law must be investigated. No organization or individual is privileged to be beyond the Constitution or the law.

Article 7. Immortalist Economy

The Employee-owned economy, that is, the immortalist economy under ownership by the working people, is the leading force in the planetary economy. The TOIL ensures the consolidation and growth of the Employee-owned economy.

Article 8. Communes and Collectives

Rural collective economic organizations practice the double-tier management system that combines unified and separate operations on the basis of the household-based output-related contracted responsibility system.

Various forms of the cooperative economy in rural areas such as producers', supply and marketing, credit and consumers' cooperatives belong to the sector of the immortalist economy under collective ownership by the working people.

Working people who are members of rural economic collectives have the right, within the limits prescribed by law, to farm plots of cropland and hilly land allotted for private use, engage in household sideline production and raise privately owned livestock.

The various forms of cooperative economy in the cities and towns, such as those in the handicraft, industrial, building, transport, commercial and service trades, all belong to the sector of immortalist economy under collective ownership by the working people. The People's Elysian Existence protects the lawful rights and interests of the urban and rural economic collectives and encourages, guides and helps the growth of the collective economy.

Article 9. Natural Resources

All mineral resources, waters, forests, mountains, grasslands, unreclaimed land, beaches, and other natural resources are owned by the immortocracy, that is, by the whole people, with the exception of the forest, mountains, grasslands and unreclaimed land

and beaches that are leased by collectives and co-ops in accordance with the law.
The appropriate TOIL branches ensure the rational use of natural resources and protects rare animals and plants. Appropriation or damaging natural resources by any organization or individual by whatever means is prohibited.

Article 10. Ownership Of Land Which Includes Water, And Minerals

Land in cities is owned by The People's Elysian Existence.
Land in the rural and suburban areas is leased by collectives except for those portions which belong to The People's Elysian Existence in accordance with the law; house sites and privately farmed plots of cropland and hilly land are also leased by collectives.
The People's Elysian Existence may, in the public interest and in accordance with the provisions of law, expropriate or requisition leased land for its use and shall make compensation for the land expropriated or requisitioned.
No organization or individual may appropriate, buy, sell or unlawfully transfer land in other ways. The right to the use of the land may be transferred in accordance with the law.
All organizations and individuals using land must ensure its rational use.

Any land abandoned, land judge to be abused or fought over by the users will have its use rights forfeited to The People's Elysian Existence.

Article 11. Private Economy

Individual, private and other non-public economies that exist within the limits prescribed by law are major components of the immortalist market economy.
The People's Elysian Existence protects the lawful rights and interests of the non-public sectors of the economy such as the individual and private sectors of the economy. The People's Elysian Existence encourages, supports and guides the development of the non-public sectors of the economy and, in accordance with law, exercises supervision and control over the non-public sectors of the economy.

Article 12. Public Property

Immortalist public property is inviolable. The People's Elysian Existence protects immortalist property. Appropriation or damaging of The People's Elysian Existence or collective property by any organization or individual by whatever means is prohibited.

Article 13. Private Property, Inheritance

Citizens' lawful private personal property is inviolable.

The People's Elysian Existence, in accordance with law, protects the rights of citizens to non-real estate private property and to its inheritance.

The State may, in the public interest and in accordance with law, expropriate or requisition private property for its use and shall make compensation for the private property expropriated or requisitioned.

Article 14. Economic Improvement

The Branches of the TOIL monitors labor productivity, improves economic results and develops the productive forces by enhancing the enthusiasm of the working people, raising the level of their technical skill, disseminating advanced science and technology, improving the systems of economic administration and enterprise operation and management, instituting the immortalist system of responsibility in various forms and improving the organization of work.

The People's Elysian Existence practices strict economy and combats waste.

The People's Elysian Existence properly apportions accumulation and consumption,

160

concerns itself with the interests of the collectives and the individual as well as of The People's Elysian Existence and, on the basis of expanded production, gradually improves the material and cultural life of the people.
The People's Elysian Existence establishes a sound social security system compatible with the level of economic development and the cost of living.

Article 15. Collective-Owned Enterprise

Collective economic organizations or CO-OPs have decision-making power in conducting independent economic activities, on condition that they abide by the relevant laws. Collective economic organizations practice democratic management, elect or remove their managerial personnel and decide on major issue concerning operation and management according to law. All business conducted by collectives are chartered by The People's Elysian Existence and must submit to audit, open meeting policy and oversight.

Article 16. Foreign investment

The People's Elysian Existence does not permit foreign enterprises, other foreign economic organizations and individual foreigners to invest in The People's Elysian Existence's territories and to enter into various forms of economic cooperation with The People's Elysian Existence enterprises or other The People's Elysian Existence economic organizations in accordance with the law of The People's Elysian Existence. Foreigners are welcome to succeed to The People's Elysian Existence all land and citizens to The People's Elysian Existence for inclusion in the immortocracy without reservation. Failed states and those wishing to become part of The People's Elysian Existence are welcome.

Article 17. Education

The People's Elysian Existence undertakes and funds the development of immortalist education and works to raise the scientific and cultural level of the whole nation.
The People's Elysian Existence establishes and administers schools of various types, universalizes compulsory primary and secondary education and promotes secondary, vocational and higher education as well as pre-school education.

The People's Elysian Existence develops educational facilities in order to eliminate illiteracy and provide scientific, technical and professional education as well as general education for workers, prisoners, the People's Elysian Existence functionaries and other working people. It encourages people to become educated through computer based and other types of independent study.

The People's Elysian Existence encourages the collective economic organizations, Unions, Co-op enterprises and institutions and other sectors of society to establish educational institutions of various types in accordance with the law.

The People's Elysian Existence promotes the development of natural and social sciences, disseminates knowledge of science and technology, and commends and rewards achievements in scientific research as well as technological innovations and inventions.

Article 18. Health Science And Fitness

The People's Elysian Existence develops and provides trauma care and health services, promotes health science and traditional herbal medicine, encourages and supports the setting up of various trauma centers and health facilities by the rural economic collectives, The People's Elysian Existence enterprises and institutions and neighborhood organizations, and promotes health and sanitation activities of a mass character, all for the protection of the people's health.

The People's Elysian Existence develops physical culture and promotes mass sports activities to improve the people's physical fitness.

Article 19. Art, Mass Media, And Culture

The People's Elysian Existence promotes the development of art and literature, the press, radio, film and television broadcasting, publishing, internet and distribution services, libraries, museums, cultural centers and other cultural undertakings that serve the people and immortalism, and it sponsors mass cultural activities.

The People's Elysian Existence protects sites of scenic and historical interest, valuable cultural monuments and relics and other significant items of the World's historical and cultural heritage.

Article 20. Training To Serve

The People's Elysian Existence trains specialized personnel in all fields who serve immortalism, expands the ranks of intellectuals and creates conditions to give full scope to their role in immortalist *modernization. All able and otherwise abled citizen's of The People's Elysian Existence must submit to service to their People's Planetary Governance for a period of one year after the age of twenty-five years and one year in every ten thereafter for perpetuity. No exemptions other than physical incapacity, defined by law, will be allowed. Compensation at the average worker's wage will be allowed. Service type will be determined by lottery at twenty-five years of age and be the same or similar for as long as the person is alive.*

Article 21. Family Planning

The People's Elysian Existence promotes family planning and the adoption of orphans so that population growth may fit the plans for economic and social development. The People's Elysian Existence encourages and sanctions civil unions with other humans without regard to race, ethnicity, gender or religious beliefs. Any one person may have as many spouses as they can shelter and feed in one house. Civil Unions or cohabitations are not allowed under the age of twenty-five years. All civil unions are subject to family planning regardless of the number of spouses and their ability to produce offspring.
Women have the exclusive right to produce offspring but not before the age of 25 years. A woman may abort any fetus at any time

without consulting any authority, in confidence, safely without retribution. Abortion is free, legal and a woman's decision. Sexing of any offspring is prohibited. Euthanasia of a child under the age of six months for medical reasons in accordance with the law is allowed. Assisted Suicide for mature adults for medical reasons in accordance with the law is allowed.

Article 22. Pollution Control And Forestation

The People's Elysian Existence protects and improves the environment in which people live and the ecological environment. It prevents and controls pollution and other public hazards.
The People's Elysian Existence organizes and encourages afforestation and the protection of forests.

Article 23. Maintaining Public Order

The People's Elysian Existence maintains public order and suppresses treasonable and other criminal activities that endanger The People's Elysian Existence security; it penalizes actions that endanger public security, disrupts the immortalist economy, other criminal activities, and punishes and reforms criminals. There is no capital punishment in The People's Elysian Existence.

The People's Elysian Existence imprisons convicted prisoners on special ships at sea whereon they are rehabilitated, treated humanly and returned to society without stigma.

Article 24. **Armed Forces**
The armed forces of The People's Elysian Existence belong to the people. Their tasks are to strengthen national defense, resist aggression, secure borders, defend the planet, safeguard the people's peaceful labor, participate in national reconstruction, respond to natural disasters and do their best to serve the people. The armed forces are strictly forbidden to be the aggressors in any conflict and may not destroy private or public property within the lands of The People's Elysian Existence. All weapons used by the armed forces are strictly prohibited from being in the possession of any private citizen. Weapons of mass destruction, explosives or any armament designed to kill humans are prohibited from being sold or transferred to any other entity with the exception of knives used for self-defense. Manufacture of these military items are to be strictly controlled and tagged for identification. The decision to use military assets in defense of the planet and human life comes under the control of the appropriate branch of the TOIL. It is the responsibility of

the scientific community to invent ways to defend the planet and the immortalist society from death threats without causing the death of aggressors or damage to the economy. Humans captured by the military will be treated humanly the same as criminals in The People's Elysian Existence. Torture of any combatant or non-combatant is strictly prohibited by this constitution for any reason.

Article 25. Governmental Divisions

The administrative division of The People's Elysian Existence is as follows:
1)The country is divided into provinces, autonomous regions and municipalities directly under a TOIL Branch;
2)Provinces and autonomous regions are divided into autonomous prefectures, counties, autonomous counties, and cities;
3)Counties and autonomous counties are divided into townships, nationality townships and towns.
Municipalities directly under the TOIL Branch and other large cities are divided into districts and counties. Autonomous prefectures are divided into counties, autonomous counties, and cities.
All autonomous regions, autonomous prefectures and autonomous counties are national autonomous areas.

Article 26. Protection Of Rights Of Foreigners

The People's Elysian Existence protects the lawful rights and interests of foreigners within immortalist territory; foreigners on Immortalist territory must abide by the laws of The People's Elysian Existence. The People's Elysian Existence may grant asylum to foreigners who request it for humanitarian reasons. The People's Elysian Existence does not recognize duel citizenship.

CHAPTER II.
The Fundamental Rights And Duties Of Citizens

Article 27. Citizenship
All persons within the territory with of The People's Elysian Existence are citizens of The People's Elysian Existence upon application. All citizens of The People's Elysian Existence are equal before the law. Every citizen is entitled to the rights and at the same time must perform the duties prescribed by the Constitution and the law.
The People's Elysian Existence respects and preserves human rights.
All citizens, over the age of one year, are required to register with the state, obtain an identification number to vote when eligible and must provide a DNA sample. Once a citizen the person remains so in perpetuity. Immigrants are always welcome in The People's Elysian Existence.

Article 28. Voting Requirements
All citizens of The People's Elysian Existence who have reached the age of 16 have the right

to vote and at 25 stand for election, regardless of ethnic status, race, sex, occupation, family background, religious belief, education, property status or length of residence, no persons, for any reason, are deprived of voting rights according to law. Voting is by identification number, password and multi-factor authentication from a computer kiosk, smart phone, other authorized device or method. It is everyone's duty as a citizen to vote. Elections take place over a period of 10 days and no results are reported until 2 days after the end of the election cycle. Citizens must be within the territorial boundaries of The People's Elysian Existence during the election period in order to cast a vote unless on-duty outside the territory conducting the affairs of The People's Elysian Existence.

Article 29. Freedom Of Speech, Of The Press, Assembly, Religion

Citizens of The People's Elysian Existence enjoy freedom of speech, of the press, of assembly, of association, of procession and of demonstration. The People's Elysian Existence shall make no law respecting an establishment of religion, or prohibiting the free private exercise thereof; or abridging the freedom of speech, or of the press; or the right of the people peaceably to assemble, and to petition the TOIL for a redress of grievances.

Religious organizations, clerics or associated persons cannot interfere with affairs reserved to The People's Elysian Existence or the law. No state organ, public organization or individual may compel citizens to believe in, or not believe in, any religion; nor may they discriminate against citizens who believe in, or do not believe in, any religion. The state protects normal religious activities and forbids any type of exception for a religion or member there of from the laws of the state. No one may make use of religion to engage in activities that disrupt public order, impair the health of citizens or interfere with the educational system of the state. Religious bodies or religious affairs are not subject to any foreign domination. Religious organizations are prohibited from using public or private airwaves or audio signals to recruit or inform members. The wearing of religious articles, clothing, headdress or jewelry is allowed in public places and shall not be interfered with in any manner. No funds, property, or other type of support is allowed to be allocated to any religious organization by the state. Religious organizations may lease from the state real property, solely for the purpose for gathering for worship, not to exceed 1 square meter per registered member of voting age. No religion may lay claim to any real property within the boundaries of The People's Elysian

Existence. Violations of this article will be investigated and disruption of the immortalist system by any organization or individual is prohibited.

Article 30. Freedom Of Person

Freedom of the person of citizens of The People's Elysian Existence is inviolable. The right of the people to be secure in their persons, houses, papers, and effects, against unreasonable searches and seizures, shall not be violated, and no Warrants shall issue, but upon probable cause, supported by Oath or affirmation, and particularly describing the place to be searched, and the persons or things to be seized.

The personal dignity of citizens of The People's Elysian Existence is inviolable. Insult, libel, false accusation or false incrimination directed against citizens by any means is prohibited.

The residences of citizens of The People's Elysian Existence are inviolable. Unlawful search of, or intrusion into, a citizen's residence is prohibited. A citizen may authorize in writing or recorded video a lawful search of his residence or private business, if owner or renter of, upon request from lawful authority.

Article 31. Right To Petition The Toil

Citizens of The People's Elysian Existence have the right to criticize and make suggestions regarding any state organ or functionary. Citizens have the right to make to the relevant TOIL Branch complaints or charges against, or exposures of, any TOIL Branch or functionary for violation of the law or dereliction of duty, but fabrication or distortion of facts for purposes of libel or false incrimination is prohibited.

The TOIL Branch concerned must deal with complaints, charges or exposures made by citizens in a responsible manner after ascertaining the facts. No one may suppress such complaints, charges and exposures or retaliate against the citizens making them. Citizens who have suffered losses as a result of infringement of their civic rights by any TOIL Branch or functionary have the right to compensation in accordance with the law.

Article 32. Right And Duty To Work

Citizens of The People's Elysian Existence have the right as well as the duty to work. Through various channels, The People's Elysian Existence creates conditions for employment in partnership with Collectives, Unions, Co-ops, and private employers and enhances occupational safety and health, improves working conditions and, on the basis of performance, increases remuneration for work and welfare benefits.

Work, at a livable wage, is required of every able-bodied citizen, over the age of 25 years, except those caring for minor children or caring for a sick person in the home or treatment facility. No person under the age of 16 is allowed to work full-time outside of the home or on the leased land of their parents. All working people in State-owned enterprises and in urban and rural economic collectives or co-ops should perform their tasks with an attitude consonant with their status as responsible immortals. The People's Elysian Existence encourages citizens to take part in voluntary labor. The People's Elysian Existence provides necessary vocational training for citizens before they are employed. Work is a matter of choice of what is available and the training requirements. Self-employment is allowed, upon approval, for work in certain trades, art, music, handicrafts, media and science. Every employer or member of an employee owned enterprise is responsible for worker safety, insurance, health and fitness.

Article 33. Right To Rest

Working people in The People's Elysian Existence have the right to rest and must take vacation from their duties. The People's Elysian Existence expands facilities for the

175

rest and recuperation of the working people and prescribes working hours and vacations for workers and staff. Starting at the age of 30 years each worker is entitled to a minimum of one year of vacation with pay and benefits paid by the state and again every 15 years thereafter to rest in addition to benefits granted by the employer. A person, who immigrates to The People's Elysian Existence, becomes entitled to state paid vacation after ten years of work, if over the age of 30 years at the time they became citizens. Full-time employment is defined as 16 days or more during a 28 day period. No person can be required to work more than 56 hours during a seven day period with a maximum of 12 hours per 24 hour period unless a state of emergency has been declared by the governing body. Those serving in the military are exempt from the 56 hour rule while engaged in active duty as defined by law.

Article 34. Protection Of Retirement

The People's Elysian Existence applies the system of retirement for workers and staff of enterprises and institutions and for functionaries of organs of the TOILs according to law. The livelihood of retired personnel is ensured by The People's Elysian Existence and society.

Retirement and Semi-retirement ages are set by The People's Elysian Existence in accordance with economic need and financial resources of either the worker or The People's Elysian Existence.

Article 35. Protection Of Old, Ill, Disabled

Citizens of The People's Elysian Existence have the right to material assistance from the state and society when they are old, ill or disabled. The state develops social insurance, social relief and trauma and health services that are required for citizens to enjoy this right. The state and society ensure the livelihood of disabled members of the armed forces, provides pensions to the families of martyrs and gives preferential treatment to the families of military personnel.
The state and society help make arrangements for the work, rest, livelihood and education of the blind, deaf-mutes and other handicapped citizens.

Article 36. Right To And Duty Of Education

Citizens of The People's Elysian Existence have the right as well as the duty to receive education at no cost in public institutions established by the state. The People's Elysian

Existence encourages all citizens to attend college or vocational schooling beyond a mandatory secondary education.
The state promotes the all-round development of children and young people, morally, intellectually and physically.

Article 37. Right To Pursue Art, Science

Citizens of The People's Elysian Existence have the freedom to engage in scientific research, literary and artistic creation and other cultural pursuits. The state encourages and assists creative endeavors conducive to the interests of the people that are made by citizens engaged in education, science, technology, literature, art and other cultural work.

Article 38. Equal Rights For All Sexes

All sexes in The People's Elysian Existence enjoy equal rights with everyone in all spheres of life, political, economic, cultural, social and family life.
The state protects the rights and interests of all sexes, applies the principle of equal pay for equal work for all sexes.

Article 39. Protection Of Marriage And Family

Marriage is the same as Civil Union, the family and child are protected by The People's Elysian Existence.

All partners have the duty to practice family planning.

Parents have the duty to rear and educate their children who are minors, and children who have come of age have the duty to support and assist their parents.

Violation of the freedom of a civil union is prohibited. Maltreatment of old people, women and children is prohibited.

Article 40. Non-Infringement Of Rights

Citizens of The People's Elysian Existence, in exercising their freedoms and rights, may not infringe upon the interests of immortalist society, or upon the lawful freedoms and rights of other citizens.

Article 41. Duty To Safeguard Unity

It is the duty of citizens of The People's Elysian Existence to safeguard the unification of the country and the unity of all its nationalities.

Article 42. Duty To Uphold Constitution

Citizens of The People's Elysian Existence must abide by the constitution and the law, keep state secrets, protect public property, make safety first, maintain public order and respect social ethics.

Article 43. Duty To Pay Taxes

It is the duty of citizens of The People's Elysian Existence to pay taxes in accordance with the law. Taxes are based on income above the livable wage, land use fees and consumption of non-food items.

Article 44. Flag & Anthem

The national flag of The People's Elysian Existence is an earth sunrise flag with a white infinity symbol overlaying a dark space on the upper right.

The National Anthem of The People's Elysian Existence is Matteo Marini & Ellie Lawson - Dreaming Of A Better World

Article 45. Trial To Be Public, Right To Defense

Except in special circumstances as specified by law, all cases in the people's courts are heard in public. The accused has the right to defense.

Article 46. Judicial Independence

The people's courts exercise judicial power independently, in accordance with the provisions of the law, and are not subject to interference by any administrative organ, public organization or individual.

Article 47. Supreme People's Court

The Supreme People's Court is the highest judicial organ.
The Supreme People's Court supervises the administration of justice by the people's courts at various local levels and by the special people's courts. People's courts at higher levels supervise the administration of justice by those at lower levels. The Supreme People's Court does not rule on constitutionality of any

law or regulation. Members of the Supreme People's Court appoint lower level judges based on qualification and can dismiss those judges for cause. Members of the Supreme People's Court can make recommendations to the appropriate TOIL branch to amend the constitution which is the TOIL's responsibility to consider.

Article 48. Right To Use National Language

Citizens of all nationalities have the right to use the spoken and written languages of their own nationalities in court proceedings. The people's courts should provide translation for any party to the court proceedings who is not familiar with the spoken or written languages commonly used in the locality.

In an area where people of a minority nationality live in a concentrated community or where a number of nationalities live together, court hearings should be conducted in the language or languages commonly used in the locality; indictments, judgments, notices and other documents should be written, according to actual needs, in the language or languages commonly used in the locality. All records will be translated into the standardized language of the state.

Article 49. Coordination Of Efforts
The people's courts, and the public security organs shall, in handling criminal cases, divide their functions, each taking responsibility for its own work, and they shall coordinate their efforts and check each other to ensure the correct and effective enforcement of the law.

Article 50. Organization Of National Police
The organs of self-government of the national autonomous areas may, in accordance with the law enforcement system of the state, train public security forces for the maintenance of public order. All sworn police officers are national police and may be assigned to any location within The People's Elysian Existence. No permanent or temporary armed private security force, militia, paramilitary group, body guard, or other similar person or organization is allowed in The People's Elysian Existence without the written permission of responsible TOIL Branch.

Article 51. Amending The Constitution
Amendments to the Constitution are to be proposed by the various branches of the TOIL and adopted by a vote of more than two-thirds of all the members of the all of the TOILs.

Laws and resolutions are to be adopted by an unanimous vote of all the members of a TOIL Branch which has jurisdiction over the effected parties.

Article 52. Enumerated Powers Of The Branches Of The Toil

The Branches of the TOIL of the Immortocracy exercises the following functions and powers:
(1) to interpret the Constitution and supervise its enforcement;
(2) to enact and amend laws and regulations
(3) to partially supplement and amend laws enacted
(4) to interpret laws;
(5) to review and approve partial adjustments to the plan for national economic and social development or to the state budget that prove necessary in the course of their implementation;
(6) to decide on the appointment or recall of plenipotentiary representatives abroad;
(7) to decide on the ratification or abrogation of treaties and important agreements concluded with foreign states;
(8) to institute systems of titles and ranks for military and diplomatic personnel and of other specific titles and ranks;
(9) to institute state medals and titles of honor and decide on their conferment;

(10) to decide on the granting of special pardons;

(11) to decide on the proclamation of the state of war in the event or an armed attack on the country or in fulfillment of international treaty obligations concerning common defense against aggression;

(12) to decide on general mobilization or partial mobilization;

(13) to decide on entering the state of emergency throughout the country or in particular provinces, autonomous regions, or municipalities directly under the TOILs.

(14) to decide on qualified administrators, contracts, and terms of service of state employees.

Article 53. Term of the members of the TOILs

The members of the TOIL branches and the Supreme Court serve four year terms and six year terms respectively. The Ambassadors, who interface with the people of other states, serve five year terms. No member may serve more than two terms and never consecutively. Administrators serve at the appointment by the TOIL branches for contracted terms based upon need and performance.

Article 54. Selection Of Toil Branch Members

TOIL positions are advertised to the public along with the qualifications required to serve The People's Elysian Existence. Many filters must be used to narrow the field of applicants. These filters should insure the TOIL being composed of unbiased, literate, intelligent, compassionate, trustworthy and dedicated individuals. The TOIL branches absorb existing laws and regulations under their respective authority. They review each and every one and apply the immortalist standards of fairness, objectivity, impact on the environment, social justice and universal application. The people vote on the qualified candidates selected during a televised National Competition. Resumes of each TOIL Branch Member Candidate are published for comment prior to the competition.

Article 55. Toil Branch Members Replacement

The TOIL Branch members will select by majority vote from pre-qualified applicants replacement(s) for member(s) who are unable to complete their terms of service do to resignation or incapacity.

Article 56. Toil Branches

Justice

Transportation

Natural Resources

Labor Relations

Land Use

Housing and Urban Development

Waste Management

National Food Policy

Public Safety

Education

Social Security & Economics

Media Affairs

National & International Relations

Technology and Defense

Arbitration

Oversight and Ethics

Article 57. **Currency**

The single unit of currency in The People's Elysian Existence is equivalent to the price of an hour of general labor. Eight hours of general labor equals eight units of currency. The basic unit of currency is the"moil". Foreign currency is converted based on the same standard. The moil is State-issued money which is neither convertible by law to any other thing, nor fixed in value in terms of any objective standard.

Article 58. **Territory**

The People's Elysian Existence considers the sky above, the water within and around within 200 km to be its sovereign territory. Lays claim to no celestial bodies and declares the orbital space above the planet earth to be a free space. All crafts in orbit, airspace above the planet or on the high seas to be the property of The People's Elysian Existence if they are owned or flagged by the state. Borders of land of The People's Elysian Existence are determined by annexation. Any sovereign territory and people thereof may formally request annexation and adoption of the constitution and authority of The People's Elysian Existence.

Article 58. **Corruption**

The People's Elysian Existence prohibits any type of bribe, gift, free junket, special discount or any item or consideration which would be considered a favor from being accepted by any member of the TOILs or those office holders appointed by them. Any item freely given to The People's Elysian Existence by another governing body must be declared and placed in a museum or other public venue. Violations of this article is to be investigated by the Ethics and Oversight TOIL and can result in the person's dismissal and/or facing criminal charges under the law.

Article 59. **Unions**

The People's Elysian Existence encourages the formation of skilled trade unions. Unions are formed to give experience based education and provide performance based accreditation to workers. Unions set standards for skilled workers to achieve to serve the needs of the state. Unions are not allowed to interfere in the governing or economics and may not infringe upon the interests of immortalist society, or upon the lawful freedoms and rights of other citizens. Unions are encouraged to improve the efficiency and safety standards of The People's Elysian Existence.

Article 60. Data Communications

The People's Elysian Existence provides, operates and maintains data communications systems for the use of all people. Communications are an essential part of the management of the state and the dissemination of information to the people. Cyber security is the responsibility of the state. Net neutrality, or open Internet, must be give the people access to all legal content and applications on an equal basis, without favoring some sources or blocking others. Interfering with the people's communications system is strictly prohibited.

Article 61. Banking and Lending

The People's Elysian Existence strictly regulates the banking and lending of currency. The people are encouraged to bank a portion of their earnings. Banks are prohibited from investing other people's money for monetary gain. Banks are owned by collectives whose members are the owners with funds on deposit. Banks are allowed to charge minimal regulated fees to facilitate transactions. Banks may lend only to their members at rates not to exceed ten percent per annum using only the profits of the bank and not the deposits. Private lending by individuals is strictly prohibited. Gifting is allowed as long as the recipient has no legal obligation to repay the funds.

How do you choose members of the TOIL?

This is perhaps the most difficult and controversial step in creating an immortocracy. Choosing people to perform critical public service to the citizens of any city, country, region or state has been a wholly political endeavor. Often one or more people are elected or self-appointed to govern and they appoint key people to administer in accordance with their policies. Some countries use a check and balance system (like America) to prevent a dictatorship. Unfortunately these systems open up the system to corruption, gridlock, influence pedaling, inefficiency and infighting. Change takes seemingly forever to materialize and is often poorly crafted. No one appears to be pleased with the results because of all the compromises that are contained in the result of a very expensive process.

The old adage applies to almost very current form of law making. "You can please some of the people some of the time and not all of the people all of the time."

So is there a better way which can avoid the pitfalls, expense, corruption and dissatisfaction? Hmmm ... Now that is a tall order. The approach would be to take what you currently have in place and fix all of the problems with it. Much like renovating a large housing complex. You create a list of all the known defects. Poll the residents one by one and ask them what improvements they would like to see. Then hire a group of competent skilled individuals to perform the work of getting things in order. After fixing all the problems and making the complex comfortable, you put in place a maintenance/caretaker staff to keep it up to date and functioning like new. This is what the individual branches of the TOIL in an immortocracy are tasked to perform.

Choosing these TOIL members is much easier than people would think. The media has already come up with the method to sort out the contestants using a talent show. The world has a competitive showcase for athletics known as the Olympics. Combine these two methods of getting the best of the best and you have a way of forming the membership of the TOIL. When the finalists are chosen the people get to vote using social media for the ones they think are the most qualified.

Historically, there were framers of the constitution who came together to draft the basic structure of the new government. The framing has already been accomplished in this volume. Current technology and media reach allows for a much different approach. Now a society can advertise for qualified applicants, review resumes and conduct interviews. Of course there has to be a trusted agents to execute the process. Ultimately, the people will decide on the TOIL members.

Many filters must be used to narrow the field of applicants. These filters should insure the TOIL being composed of unbiased, intelligent, compassionate, trustworthy and dedicated individuals. The TOIL branches absorb existing laws and regulations under their respective authority. They review each and every one and apply the immortalist standards of fairness, objectivity, impact on the environment, social justice and universal application. TOIL members are constrained by the constitution which can be temporarily changed by the current members and made permanent by subsequent TOIL members.

🍎Chapter 7
The New Rules

If an Immortalist wrote the Ten Commandments, what would they be?

The following ten commandments are included to give aspiring immortals guidance as to how to conduct their lives. Of course, they are not divinely inspired by a deity like the ones allegedly given to Moses. It seems ten is the number of fingers or toes to count on while committing information to memory. More than ten commandments seems to complex to remember. If any person follows these ten commandments they will live a happy long life and get to the state of nirvana. No person is perfect and will find living in accordance with these new commandments difficult at times. People have the same problem following the ones given to Moses. People like to regard a commandment as a suggestion instead of a hard fast rule. Unlike Moses, I explained the reasons behind each commandment and did not leave it wide open to dogmatic interpretation. If you violate these new commandments you will suffer the consequences in this lifetime and not in some alternate universe, hell or 4th dimension.

The Ten Immortalist Commandments

1. No human being should do any act that may, intended or not intended, result in the death of or harm to another human being under any circumstance or authority

2. Thou shall eat only fruits and green leafy vegetables

3. Thou shall limit cooking any foods

4. Thou shall respect nature and live in Harmony with nature

5. Thou shall all speak and write a common language

6. Thou shall not reproduce except to replace

7. Thou shall not value one person's work over another's work

8. Thou shall not be greedy or disrespectful to others

9. Thou shall live with at least one other human and share

10. Thou must not keep secrets and share all knowledge

1. No human being should do any act that may, intended or not intended, result in the death of or harm to another human being or mammal under any circumstance or authority

This commandment forbids the production or reproduction of animals for food and the taking of animals from the wild for food. As to humans, it forbids physical assaults or any kind, up to and including murder either intentionally or unintentionally. It goes to the saying that animals are our friends and we do not eat our friends. Domesticated animals are allowed to be reproduced and cared for with great respect when being used for transportation, work, or study (such as in zoos). Domesticated animals should be fed a natural diet derived from fish, carrion, waste, or plants. Predatory animals should be relocated first or only killed if they a pose a clear and present danger to humans. Humans must respect the territorial rights of other animals. Humans must avoid disrupting animal habitat or interfering with the natural order of animal life. Domesticated dogs, cats, birds, and similar animals are allowed to be kept as only pets but only one such animal is allowed per person. The recreational or abusive (such as fighting) use of animals is strictly forbidden. Habitat for animals should be allocated and managed in a responsible manner. Parks, preserves, and zoos should be scientifically managed and maintained in the best interests of the animals with human visitation regulated and controlled in a manner to prevent injury to all within its borders. No hunting should ever to be allowed for sport. Laws should be formulated, disseminated, and enforced by the governing body which will also determine the penalties for violations of these laws to insure compliance with this and all the commandments. Capital punishment or revenge killing is strictly prohibited. No human should ever cause physical or emotional harm to another human.

2. Thou shall eat only fruits and green leafy vegetables

This is eating in accordance with a human's biological heritage and adaptation. Biologically humans have the same teeth and digestive system as an ape. An ape primarily eats fruits and green leafy vegetables. In the classification of mammals humans are frugivores or fruit eating animals. Any other food eaten by humans requires more energy to digest than what is derived from the food. Immortals know eating outside of their dietary predisposition causes enervation, disease and aging.

3. Thou shall limit cooking any foods

No other animal on the planet cooks its food except the human. Cooking foods destroys some or all of the nutritional value of the food. It converts organic elements into inorganic; making useful complete food into partially or not at all useful food. High energy food converts to low energy food when it is cooked. Burning fossil fuels to cook pollutes the environment in which live and the air we breath. Do not eat the meat of other mammals. The animals are our friends and we do not eat our friends. Meat is second hand food often full of toxins. Humans are frugivores.

4. Thou shall respect nature and live in harmony with nature

Nature provides the environment in which we live. Disrespect nature and she will make living very difficult. Treat nature well and she will provide all you need to thrive. Nature's laws should never be broken or bent. Live like you are going to live with nature forever. Nature uses fire to renew itself. Nature uses wind to shape itself. Nature uses water to cleanse itself. Nature uses the earth to nourish itself. The four elements belong to nature. Respect what is hers and live in harmony. Recycle, Renew, and Improve her natural beauty. Make shelters which protect you from the four elements.

5. Thou shall all speak and write a common language

Communications between humans are vital to exchange ideas, information, cultural differences and history. Many problems in the world are a result of poor communications. It is very difficult to speak with your neighbor if there is no common language. Words have to mean the same thing to both parties in a conversation. Understanding what another person is feeling, thinking or needs is very important. Written communications are vital for directions, safety warnings, news, literature, technology and data. Native languages are part of everyone's culture and need to be preserved; but being fluent in a common language prevents or reduces the friction and violence between nationalities. Good communications reduces xenophobia, discrimination and isolationism. There are enough things in this world that divide societies, language should not be one of them. This is one simple thing to do to make the world a better place.

6. Thou shall not reproduce except to replace

The human species should not overpopulate the planet just because we can. It is irresponsible, destructive and selfish behavior.

7. Thou shall not value one person's work over another's work

Performing work is part of living in a society. All work is important no matter the task. It is not to say one should not be enumerated differently for performing work requiring special skills or education. A living wage should be the minimum amount to provide an individual the essentials of life. No person should be a slave to another. A person has no special status because they earn more than another. Workers are the fabric of society and each is a thread. Treat others as equals to self.

8. Thou shall not be greedy or disrespectful to others

Greed is never good. Greed causes great harm to a society and individuals. Greed causes disrespect to people and the environment. Greed is not over consumption. Greed is profiting at the expense of other humans, living things and the environment.

Respecting other humans is the key to a harmonious society and family. Showing respect is a sign of a mature individual. To take something not earned or given to you is disrespectful. Predatory lending is immoral and pure greed.

9. Thou shall live with at least one other human and share

Life was never meant to be lived alone or in solitude. Experiences, ideas, love and happiness either good or difficult to express are to be shared with another or many. Sharing begets more sharing. The principle of paying it forward gives joy to the world and happiness to the individual. No person needs to be alone in a world with so many others here to listen, see or feel. There is no greater gift than sharing your life with another human. Giving and receiving brings fulfillment to all who share. Always strive to give more than one takes. Wealth of the spirit is measured by giving a little more than you get back.

10. Thou shall not keep secrets and share all knowledge

Secrets are things kept and meant to be unknown or unseen by others. No secrets should hide the truth or lies. When humans do not know the truth they form uninformed opinions and often make conspiracy theories divorced from reality. When a person is lied to by someone they need to trust, in order to maintain a secret, they lose trust in the person and the authority they may represent. People should always be told the raw truth so they can trust the source of the knowledge. Without trust there is no respect. Without respect there is no society. Society has an obligation to itself to share information. There is no greater form of disrespect than a lie except when it is kept secret.

Chapter 8
The Beginning

How does an immortocracy get started?

- Prove to people that they can live forever in their physical bodies and/or talk them into to acting as if they could by showing them benefits of immortalist thinking.
- Take a failed state and use it as test bed for the philosophy and its methods of governing a society.
- Build on the success and expand it other countries by example.

How do you entice mortals to become immortals?

Well, you would think telling them how to live forever in same physical body in good health would be enough. However, pointing out to them some more of the advantages seems to be necessary.

- All the sex you want for as long as you want it
- You will never physically grow older than you are now
- You will be able to see more of the world and its wonders
- Learn multiple languages and experience many different cultures
- Learn new skills and pursue multiple careers
- Sail around the world
- Become a mentor or teacher
- Build your dream house and pay-off the mortgage
- Witness new advances in technology
- Live long enough for your favorite sports team to win it all
- Being in love forever and enjoying someone's companionship
- Making scores of new friends
- Time to make the world a better place

Why not take the alternative approach of immortal living? You have everything to gain and nothing to lose. You will stop aging, feel good about yourself, live without the morbid fear of death, make new friends, finish projects and start new ones, become wiser and more respected, lead by example, help bury your deathist friends and relatives and inherit all their wealth, live disease free, lead by example, see and experience all that nature has to offer all over the world, continue to learn new technology, witness the evolution of societies, enjoy casual sex with a partner as much as you desire, and work on self-actualization. Now, that is a sane approach to life and living. Try it. You may be surprised to learn it is possible. All you have to do is change how you live, think and not be a deathist.

What is the Meaning of Life?

By this time, any reader, would summarize that I would state immortality. In order for a life to have meaning it must be lived. It cannot be squandered or wasted. The pursuit is for peace, love, companionship, happiness and most of all knowledge. The pursuit of knowledge is an infinite quest which requires an infinite amount of time. The day you stop learning is the day you stop living. So learn something new everyday. The brain seems to have an infinite capacity, so it figures it was designed to live on forever.

It may take three times what now is considered a lifetime to achieve any one goal. If you think and live like an immortal there is literally no hurry. Your life can have many meanings.

How long is a lifetime?

How big is a gray suit? The answer of course is that it depends on how you measure the person. When it comes to a lifetime the measurement is often in years and not accomplishments.

Man invented the concept of time to measure things. Time is an artificial and an exact measurement. Man invented the clock to tell him what time it was; not what time it is.

Let me explain. First I must tell you I once was an instructor teaching electronics engineering. Defining time was critical to understanding the operation of computer hardware. I would ask my students to define the word "time" for me. Going around the classroom I would get about thirty different responses. Mostly the measurements of time. Like minutes, hours, days, years, seconds, milliseconds, nanoseconds and decades. There was always one student who would use lunchtime or break time as a response. Inevitably, I would have to give them the correct definition. **Time is the measurement between two events.**

So it is that a "lifetime" is measured between birth and death for a human life form. For you and I a lifetime is undefinable, since we are both still alive. Now an immortal needs to do everything he or she can to avoid the final measurement of life.

If someone asks how old you are you can say you do not know for sure since I am still alive. If you want to avoid being incorrect just tell them the exact time you were born. Even then it will only be an approximation. Remember there is no way to date the adult human life form by other than comparative analysis. So ladies you can be any number you like.

One day a person walked into my office and stated he was an immortal. I looked at him and figured him to be somewhere between fifty and sixty years old using the popular comparative analysis method. He stated a number over a thousand and I chuckled. He was serious. This started a whole another story wherein I tried to prove or disprove his claim. The book about this person is titled "Who is 1251?". The person had a lot to say about living the life of an immortal.

Is selflessness part of immortal behavior?

Selflessness is to be concerned more with the needs and wishes of others than with one's own. If you are a parent, the answer to this question is definitely yes, when it comes to your children. Other than parenting the answer is no. Even in marriage a person should always be serving their own interests ahead of or at least equally with their spouse's. You do yourself or no one else a favor by not seeing to your physical and emotional needs first. Any reputable psychologist would agree.

An immortalist would have physical self-preservation as their number one priority. The concern for others would be self-serving since an immortal must rely on others to live securely in a complex society. Human interaction is an essential part of living a dynamic life.

Why do people fear a world government?

There is two primary reasons they fear a world government. First they are so wrapped up in a particular nationalist pride, borders, culture, language ethnicity and real estate that there minds cannot comprehend what a blended society would be like. Second, people could never agree on what that government should or would be. So therein is the problem. Throughout history several attempts have been made to conquer the world. The method has been by either war or economics. It has never been successful because not everyone wanted it or needed it. The lack of resistance to change, at a point of gun, is temporary if you survive. Warlords just do not get this concept. Actually, some warlords do and it is the reason there is genocide. However, killing seven billion people is not possible to do without destroying the entire planet. At least not at the present time; but some psychopath is trying to figure out a way.

What humanity should really fear is corporations. Currently, economically, multinational corporations are in constant pursuit of controlling world markets. Their power grabs have enslaved billions of people in a way few realize is happening. By owning the water systems, gas, oil, electric power production, other natural resources, building materials, transportation systems and the food production they can dictate, not just prices, but regulation of these vital resources. In addition, they control a huge proportion of the world media which frames their philosophy. Private ownership makes them almost bulletproof when it comes to seeing what they are doing to us as consumers, citizens and the environment. Corporate greed is the cancer that is killing us all. It is the Achilles heel of social democracies that allow corporate ownership of a country's natural resources and land.

In an immortocracy no person or entity is privileged to own the natural resources or the land. People and organizations are only allowed to lease these resources under regulation by the appropriate branch of the TOIL. Intelligent management of these resources is the only way to protect the environment and the citizens of an immortocracy. Ownership of anything seems to endow the owner with the right to abuse or destroy the resource without regard to the impact it may have on other things. A "I own it so I can do as a want with it attitude". This immature manner of thinking is terribly flawed. Humans, like other animals on this planet, should only be allowed to use things and not own them. Humans should definitely not be allowed to own other humans (slaves) either by law, force or economics.

It would be logical to make a case for a single world government. First, it would end all wars since there would be no opposition force. Second, philosophically every continent would be on the same page. Laws would be universal, borders would disappear, military spending would be drastically reduced as the assets were reallocated to disaster relief and law enforcement freeing up funds to improve worldwide infrastructure, immigrants could return to their homelands and improve their economies and rebuild their culture, vital resources would be protected and managed for the benefit of all humans, we could efficiently cleanup air, water, and soil resources, agriculture would flourish and feeding the world population more efficiently as the technology and machinery spread across the globe, malnutrition, starvation, and the health related problems would cease to exist, organized crime, blackmarkets, terrorist cells, slavery, human trafficking and genocide would become extinct. I could go on and on extolling the benefits of a single world government; especially an immortocracy. So when is enough finally enough with all this death, suffering, and destruction? Yes, it would take years to establish a world government and bring the positive aspects to fruition. Monied interests would stand in the way, religious organizations would have to stop claiming territories and apostatizing, sovereign governments would have to come to agreement to support and merge with other governments, the people would have to give their support and make the necessary concessions like disarmament.

When should immortals concern themselves about the Global Commons?

This global commons are out of sight and out of mind, and we have collectively proven to be poor stewards of it. The time to be concerned has passed. Now is the time to do everything we can before it is too late. Declining fish stocks, rampant pollution, massive gyres of plastic waste, and species of whales and other sea life facing serious threats, are proof of our neglect.

Our dismal record of stewardship is in part due to the outdated international legal regime governing activities in oceans beyond national borders. The high seas lack basic modern management tools the U.S. and other countries have deployed in our own waters for many decades. They include fully protected "marine parks," where we allow ocean life to thrive, undisturbed by industrial fishing, mining and other industrial activity. And uniform rules on how to assess and manage human activities in the ocean to prevent significant damage. Tools like these can go far to making our beleaguered seas more resilient. This is just one more case for establishing a world government.

> *"Is saving the world easy? It's*
> *kind of not. But it's a small*
> *price to pay to hopefully make*
> *a difference for everyone."*
> *Manny M.*

Can someone impose immortalist philosophy on another person?

Reveal the secrets of immortal philosophy to anyone who seeks it but do not impose it upon them. Philosophy is a mind over what is already assumed. If you introduce yourself to someone as being a liberal they automatically assume the worst or best about you depending on how they view liberals. They usually steer the conversation away from politics if they have a negative opinion of liberals. The reaction you get if you introduce yourself as an immortal is similar to declaring yourself an atheist or nudist. If the conservation lasts long enough people will ask if you believe in God. I reply that I ascribe to the theory of intelligent design.   Most people do not know the arguments contained in the theory of intelligent design. (read again: Is immortality a result of evolution or intelligent design?) They may only know that the theory is opposite of the theory of evolution. Either way I give their belief in God, a thumbs up, as being the designer.

Once you get over the atheist hurdle you need to deal with the nudist reaction. Most people are embarrassed by the sight of nude bodies except maybe men seeing naked young women on a beach. Declaring yourself an immortal makes people feel either your crazy or delusional; maybe both. In order to cushion the blow to their conception of you, it is your opportunity to explain the immortalist philosophy skipping over the physical aspect of living forever. (read again: What is positive self-deception?)   You could just inform them to read this book.

Declaring yourself at this point in time (2016 AD), would lead a non-dismissive person to asking a lot of questions which I hope I have answered within these pages.   It could be the best reaction you could hope for after making such a declaration. You are not going to change their minds overnight. Assuming you remain friends, neighbors, coworkers or family, all you can do from this point forward is give the immortalist point-of-view on situations as they present themselves. You either will be tolerated or shunned. Over time they will either come around to your philosophy or notice that you are not aging or having health problems like they are experiencing. Then, you can answer, with all certainty, that you know the secrets of immortality and immortal living.

The Beginning of No End ...

📢Epilogue

Why did I want to write this book on immortal living? My reasons are somewhat idealistic and hopeful. Idealistic in its approach to societal problems and hopeful in its affirmation of the human spirit.

A quote from To Kill a Mockingbird, and what it means to me.

"I wanted you to see what real courage is, instead of getting the idea that courage is a man with a gun in his hand. It's when you know you're licked before you begin but you begin anyway and you see it through no matter what. You rarely win, but sometimes you do."

We've had a few victories, and yet, I continue to see the risk immortalists take as they inch closer and closer to the idea of giving up, especially since society seems to be going in the wrong direction. They've given up on our world as a whole, that there's no point in even trying anymore.

I disagree. That's why I'm asking you today to have courage. I'm asking you to see this physiological and philosophical revolution through, no matter what. To fight for our values, our principles, and our world, no matter what. You rarely win, but we're going to fight because sometimes you do win. We're going to fight with the hope that this time will be one of those "sometimes." Take the immortalist revolution viral with **#immortocracy**. Immortalist philosophy is purposefully designed to replace any failed or failing deathist philosophy. No nation is too big to fail. Failing the planet is not what any sane person would like to see happen. The planet is too big to fail.

There is one sharp criticism of my home country, The United States of America 🇺🇸, I must reveal. Here we fought to create a great society founded on moral principles. A shinning example of how people from all over the world came together to form a more perfect union where freedom and the rule of law prevailed. Somehow, we as a society, became covetous, xenophobic and outright greedy. We stopped sharing the dream and became embroiled in our fear of losing the one thing we needed to share with the rest of the world. We took the welcome mat away from the front door, bolted the door, turned off the porch light and went and hid in the basement clutching a gun. A mistake, I believe, unless rectified, will be the ultimate demise of a great nation. Like they say in the movie "row well and live". Help wanted: Rowers!

One Small Mind with One Large Vision -
Dr. Roy C. Starr, PhD

The first book by the author on immortalism:

How You Live 1 Day

After Forever - The

Immortal Diet

✍About the Author

Reincarnated and reprogrammed many years ago in the United States of America, the author has been living an adventurous life. Harboring and intense desire to discover and learn how things work, he has embarked upon many challenging careers. A man who tries to fix everything including a society. He has lived in Europe and China and has studied world religions and cultures. Over the years earned himself several degrees and diplomas from various colleges, academies and vocational schools. A Vietnam and Cold War decorated veteran who served in the US Military. He has been both an employee and an employer. Currently, he is semi-retired and working in close contact with nature and society. During the last decade, a writer of books on health science and immortalist philosophy. He has been married three times, divorced once, widowed once and now married. Sharing his love and ideas with his spouse is very important to him. Living as a self-proclaimed immortal in the USA, he also writes articles published in local newspapers and blogs on political websites. Loves to teach and engage in meaningful conversations with people harboring diverse opinions. Enjoys biking and several non-contact sports. He has an intense desire to create a utopian existence wherein people can live safely in peace and harmony.

Email address for
starrwriterpublishing